# STRATEGIES FOR MANAGING CHANGE

## WILLIAM G. DYER

Brigham Young University

**Addison-Wesley Publishing Company, Inc.**

Reading, Massachusetts · Menlo Park, California
Don Mills, Ontario · Wokingham, England · Amsterdam · Sydney
Singapore · Tokyo · Mexico City · Bogotá · Santiago · San Juan

Library of Congress Cataloging in Publication Data

Dyer, William G.
  Strategies for managing change.
  Rev. ed. of: Insight to impact. 1976.
  Bibliography: p.
  Includes index.
  1. Social change.  2. Group relations training.
3. Social group work.  4. Organizational change.
I. Dyer, William G. Insight to impact.  I. Title.
HM101.D96  1984      303.4      84-6219
ISBN 0-201-10346-X

Cover design by Mike Fender

Text design by Laura Fredericks, Watertown, MA

Set in 10 point Palatino by Techna Type, Inc., York, PA

BCDEFGHIJ-AL-8765

*Second Printing, May 1985*

ii

# TABLE OF CONTENTS

# Preface

The issue of change is surely the most important matter facing anyone who is responsible for a human organization—be it family, business, school, church, agency, club, or association. Any unit head or manager must be concerned with improving output, attendance, quality of activity, and morale—or reducing conflict, hostility, apathy, or dissatisfaction. Managers responsible for initiating change often need assistance in planning and implementing a change program. This need has given rise to professional persons who work as consultants or change agents either inside or outside organizations to assist managers in matters of change. It is for both the manager and the professional change agent that this volume has been prepared.

The key change issue addressed here is the matter of strategy or plan. Once one identifies a problem (and all change represents a problem condition one wishes to alter), it is critical to devise a strategy that has potential to succeed and that one can implement with confidence. The appropriate strategy depends in part on whether the focus of the change attempt is an individual, a group, or a larger organizational unit.

In this book, Section 1 deals with the overall matter of developing strategies of change, regardless of the focus of interest and taking into account both ends and means. The end result one wishes to achieve is considered along with the process used to bring about the desired change. Because change is treated as a form of problem-solving, effective change programs include the important steps of data-gathering and diagnosis *before* the actual plan of action is developed. Moreover, sufficient motivation must be generated in the targets of change to ensure the plan in fact will be carried out. Any change program will experience some snags and resistance; thus, general factors that block change are examined. Finally, the ethics of the change agent and the change process are reviewed.

Section 2 addresses change that is centered on the individual or on interpersonal behaviors between people such as husband-wife, teacher-student, boss-subordinate, parent-child. This section may be of greatest interest to parents, teachers, or managers with problem employees. Some of the chapters identify goals of change, such as becoming more congruent in behavior, reducing conflict, increasing interdependence between people, and working out adjustments. Certain processes or strategies are also presented, particularly the eliciting and the giving of feedback, specific planning, developing a support system, engaging in some risk, and experiencing acceptance from others.

Section 3, in which the object of change shifts to the group and the organization, is of major concern to managers and professional change facilitators. Successful organizational change depends especially on an effective diagnosis of either the subsystems of the organization, the organization's culture, or the external environmental forces. All organizations are open systems—that is, subject to influences from the outside environment—and change strategies must take these external forces into account. Strategies for building a work team, improving creativity in the system, and changing the culture of the organization are examined. One of the great blocks to organizational change emerges when people publicly embrace a course of action but personally disagree. This matter of dysfunctional agreement is explored.

Much of this volume developed from an earlier form in the book *Insight to Impact* (Provo, Utah: Brigham Young University Press, 1972). All materials in the earlier work have been revised and updated. Several chapters are completely new. Recognition is given to Dr. Robert D. Dyer for his chapter on "Planning Individual Change," which represents a summary of the format he uses in his own training programs. Dr. W. Gibb Dyer, Jr., who completed his doctoral work at Massachusetts Institute of Technology and has been emphasizing the analysis of organization cultures, has prepared a chapter on "Culture Analysis and Change."

Special recognition and appreciation are given to Charisse Brown, who has been an important factor in the typing and production of the manuscript.

Provo, Utah                                             WILLIAM G. DYER

# SECTION ONE

# Overview of Managing Change

## Introduction

Changes in human conditions, be they societal or organizational, are going to occur. Nothing is static. The natural process of growth and decline, decay and maturation, will always cause people to make changes in conditions around them. For those in positions of management or leadership the issue is, how can we plan change with reasonable assurance that the desired consequence can be achieved? This question has lead to a great deal of research and action in the area of planned change.

This section looks at the areas of planned behavior change—at the individual, group, and organizational levels. Societal change with an emphasis on the control or use of mass media and the national political process will not be covered. Basic to any planned change strategy in the other areas is an overall theory about how change is achieved, how a motivational set towards change is created, and the kind of relationship needed between the one desiring the change (the change agent) and the person or unit that is the focus of change. This section will consider these matters, along with the ethical questions that must be considered in any change program. Ethically, anyone who tries to change another's behavior must ask: "What right do I have even to try to change another person?" Critics of modern organization development practices have charged that management has unethically tried to manipulate workers' performance to increase productivity without sharing any benefits with the workers. Any change program should examine carefully the ethical foundation of starting such a program.

# CHAPTER 1
# Changing Behavior

Almost everyone, at one time or another, wants to be a change agent—that is, he or she would like to influence someone else's behavior. Parents often want their children to stop being lazy and start helping around the house. Teachers would be delighted if students would shift their attention from sports and social activities to serious study. Managers would like to "motivate" their subordinates to increase the quantity or quality of work.

Most people have theories about how to produce such changes. Some think change is controlled through rewards and punishments. Their experience tells them that if they threaten punishment (a poor grade, a loss of privileges, or a reduced income), some people will do what they want. Although sometimes that strategy works, it also can produce arguments, resignations, or minimal change at the cost of continued underlying resentment and hostility.

Instead of threats or bribes, other people prefer to appeal to feelings of love and devotion to them personally, or to a sense of fair play ("You owe me something for all I've done for you"). Again, this strategy may generate results, but it also may produce unspoken resentment from those who feel coerced by the threat of withdrawal of love or support.

Are there strategies of change that could work without so many negative by-products? Have the researchers and thinkers in this field learned anything that would help prospective change agents face challenges with more optimism and promise of success? The answer is yes, and this volume will spell out the various factors and conditions that seem to be connected to successful change efforts. A variety of terms have been applied to the person or persons who engage in change attempts. "Change agent" will be used often here. Others may prefer the term "facilitator" or "consultant" or "OD practitioner" when referring to a professional in the change field. But one need not be a professional to engage in a change program; "change agent" defines anyone attempting to bring about a change or improvement. The term "change team" also will be used to represent the combination of a professional consultant and a concerned manager.

# Individual vs. Collective Change

The change agent may be interested in altering the performance of a specific person or in changing the rate or average performance of a group of people. If an individual is the target of change ("How can I get my son to earn better grades so he can get into college?"), the change effort may be quite different than that required for collective change ("Is it possible to improve the attendance at the meeting of our club?").

If you are trying to change the behavior of a specific person, it will be necessary to know something about that individual and gear the change plan to take into account his or her needs, goals, values, interests, background, etc. However, if the target of change is group performance (daily work output, attendance, grievance rate, breakage, turnover), the strategy will focus on the collective change of a number of people.

The issue of collective vs. individual change is one that faces many people and organizations. Officials involved with traffic safety are concerned with reducing the accident and death toll over the Christmas holidays or Labor Day weekend. At times their strategy has been effective and the death rate has been reduced. At the same time, a traffic official also may be interested in trying to insure that his own teenage child safely handles a holiday trip.

Strategies for change, whether at the individual or collective level, are always geared at people—when change occurs it is because some person has decided to alter his or her performance. Sometimes we talk and write as though there were a reality to the concept of "the organization." It is not uncommon to read "the organization had a drop in sales or production." But an organization is an abstraction—organizations don't change their behavior, although a change in organization structure or process can impact behavior. What actually occurs is that a collection of people who share common orientations consciously or unconsciously decide to lower or raise activity, or conditions prevail that make it more difficult or easier for them to perform as they had done before. A strategy to produce change is always directed at affecting human behavior.

# Group vs. Collectivity

In thinking about collective behavior, it is important to differentiate between a collection of people who are connected in some interactive way in a system called a "group" and a collection of people who share some common condition but have no group ties or interactions. Employees who work together producing a product, who talk together, plan together, and can make decisions either formally or informally, are a group. When we are among literally millions of people all driving cars over a holiday, we are part of a common collectivity but not part of a group. Strategies for change applicable to a group may not even be possible with general collectivities. For example, group members may be able to discuss an issue and influence each other, but the collectivity usually must be reached through different processes of influence such as mass media (TV, radio, written messages, etc.).

Starting with the famous Hawthorne studies around 1930 and the pioneer group research by Sherif and Ashe, there have been consistent findings that individuals can be and often are influenced in their judgments, decisions, and actions by the way group members behave toward them. Although the group may be a strong force in creating change, it is not always possible to predict the change of a *specific* group member, and group pressure is a method that cannot be used in the unconnected collectivity.

Thus, the strategy for change is dependent on the target of change—an individual, a group, or a general collectivity of people.

## A General Strategy

There is one general strategy that can be employed, regardless of the target, to determine how to arrive at a *specific* action strategy. This strategy, based on the assumption that change represents a type of problem that needs to be solved, includes the following seven steps (see Figure 1.1):

**Figure 1.1**    General Problem Solving Model

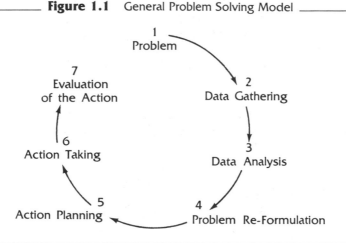

## *1. Problem Identification*

All planned change strategies begin with a condition that someone feels needs improvement. As will be discussed later, the success of the change plan will be affected to the degree that everyone involved realizes that a problem exists, defines it the same way, and agrees that improving the condition is desirable. Change programs get bogged down quickly if some people see the problem one way but others either do not admit there is a problem or see it differently. Problem identification includes a general consensus as to *why* there is a problem as well as *what* the problem is. The strategy begins with identifying the problem as clearly as possible; step four in the process allows for redefinition after some data gathering and analysis has occurred.

**CASE.** George and Helen Abrams are concerned and upset about their three children, ages 16, 14, and 11. Lately, the children have been less cooperative in helping around the home, slow to respond to requests from parents, particularly George, and reluctant to spend time on music lessons and school work. The problem as seen by the parents: Why are our children more rebellious now, and how can we make them more responsible around the house?

The Abrams children are also perplexed. As they get older, they have more and more demands made on their time. Although they are involved in school band, debate team, sports, and social activities, they are nevertheless expected to follow their parents' orders. The problem as seen by the children: Why can't our parents ease up on their demands and recognize that we can't do everything they want and remain involved in our current activities?

If we accept the viewpoint of the parents, the goal is to develop an action plan for changing the behavior of increasingly rebellious and resistant children. However, if we accept the children's perception of the situation, the issue is parents who demand more than is reasonable. The formulation presented here would allow either problem definition to be a starting point so long as data could be gathered from all parties involved. After all the data have been examined by those concerned, a re-definition of the problem, acceptable to all, can be established. A new problem statement might be: How can parents and children develop a consensus on work behavior in the home?

## *2. Data-Gathering*

Accurate data on why a problem exists is central to the creation of change. If relationships between two departments are filled with conflict, for example, some type of data-gathering procedure is necessary to ascertain from both departments why this problem exists.

There are primary and secondary sources of data. The information collected from primary sources tends to be more accurate.

*a) Primary sources of data.* The best primary source of data is direct observation. There are problems to which this method cannot be applied, but when there are complaints about a manager's performance, a teacher's competency in the classroom, or the ineffectiveness of staff meetings, it may be possible to watch the people in action.

If the problem is low attendance at meetings, one can determine directly or by reading attendance reports that people are staying away. The critical issue is, "Why?" Discovering the answer means talking to the nonattenders and asking what is blocking their involvement. Thus, interviews or written comments from those directly involved in the situation under examination constitute a primary source. If one uses the interview or the questionnaire or survey form, there always is the chance that people aren't telling the total truth. If the data-giver feels threatened by the interviewer or fears that the data may be misused to his or her detriment, the information may not be accurate. Sometimes, those in superior positions are threatening and should not be gathering data. Under such circumstances, it would be best to have an outside person (a consultant or personnel specialist) conduct the interview or survey.

*b) Secondary sources of data.* Information from secondary sources— anything other than direct observation or input from those involved— may be inaccurate. Records and reports are secondary sources that reflect reality but may be falsified, incomplete, or slanted to reflect a particular bias. An informant who has talked to someone directly involved but has not been personally involved in the problem situation is another secondary source.

Too often, managers plan action based on inadequate secondary sources of data. When a problem is raised at a management meeting, someone usually asks, "Why does the problem exist?" At that point, people supply secondary data ("What I've heard is this," or "Some people have told me . . .") that may be totally biased or inaccurate. It is wise to arrange more direct data-gathering before action is planned or taken.

## 3. Data Analysis

A helpful analysis might include some type of frequency tabulation—how many people said what, or how many times something occurred—or an intensity tabulation. In the gathering of data, it is often crucial to determine not only how often something occurs, but how strongly people feel about a particular condition. It has been often observed in surveys or interviews that people indicate that a certain action occurs rather infrequently but has strong impact when it does. One organizational study reported that workers were very threatened by the possibility of an emotional explosion from a certain key executive. Such outbursts happened only once every year or so, but the unpleasant consequences were remembered for a long time. These incidents became a part of the organization's mythology, and all newcomers heard about this particular manager.

Following the tabulation by frequency and intensity, it is useful to sort the data into three categories: a) a condition that can be altered or acted upon directly—a target of change; b) a condition that can be handled by someone whom the data-gatherer must influence; and c) unchangeable conditions that must be coped with.

**CASE.** The Intermountain Metals Company had a serious problem with its Edgemont plant, which had been in operation for a year without producing the projected output; moreover, nearly half the first-line foremen had resigned. After a major change program was instituted, a team of outside and inside change specialists spent a month gathering data. They interviewed all currently employed and former managers and administered an organization analysis survey to all current and former employees. In the data analysis phase, the information about why people quit and why they felt production was down was sorted out this way:

| **Type A Factors**<br>*Those that can be handled directly—Targets of Change* | **Type B Factors**<br>*Those someone else must handle—Targets of Influence* | **Type C Factors**<br>*Those we don't seem to be able to change—Targets for Coping* |
|---|---|---|
| 1. The production process was completed and new workers were shoved into the line before they were adequately trained. | 1. The plant was required to use certain equipment designed by people who were not located at the plant. The equipment was seen as dysfunctional. | 1. The plant was located a long way from the community where most workers live. They did not like the long commute. |
| 2. Departments were in conflict with one another, particularly production and maintenance and production and supply. | 2. The budget for training new employees was drastically cut by the corporate training department. | 3. Other companies located close to the live-in community began to hire and attract company employees. |

The data sorting shows that the Type A factors can be targets of change for the Intermountain Metals Company. Within the plant, some type of interdepartmental team building could be initiated to deal with the second

Type A problem. Solving the first Type A problem may be dependent on influencing the corporate training department to restore funds for training. Sharing with corporate headquarters new data showing that the lack of training has influenced output becomes a logical plan of action in this case.

It is not possible to move the plant close to the community or move the community close to the plant. It is possible for management to create some conditions that would allow employees to better accept the situation; e.g., paid travel time, company transportation, or proof of how company benefits compensate for the extra travel.

## 4. Problem Reformulation

Following the analysis of data, the original or presenting problem becomes refocused because of greater information. In the metals company case, the initial problems were lower-than-satisfactory production and a high turnover of personnel. Although these conditions remained the central issues, the data-gathering and analysis showed that the factors behind the presenting problems were inadequate technology on the production line, inadequately trained workers, and departmental conflicts, all of which made competitive employment opportunities more attractive. The reformulation of the problem means that the action plan should address technology, departmental conflicts, and inadequate training.

## 5. Action Planning

Having determined why the presenting problem exists, it is now possible to begin developing a plan of action to deal with the problem conditions. Table 1.1 shows a matrix of different kinds of actions or interventions that might be possible depending on the data analysis or diagnosis. If the problem is located in the social system at an intergroup level (interde-partmental conflict), the action plan should include some action that would reduce the difficulties between departments. This change matrix illustrates the types of change actions that are possible if the target of change is the individual, the group, or the larger organization. It also shows whether the change is located in the social or human system, the technical system, or the administration system, or is affected by forces outside the organization.

Action planning is often a mix of empirical and creative processes. The empirical aspect examines the types of change actions that were used in the past on similar problems and their degree of success. Sometimes there is no past experience to draw upon. The creative process addresses the kind of change action that would have the best chance of reducing or eliminating the problem.

**TABLE 1.1**
**Change Intervention Matrix**

| | Internal Systems | | Administrative System | External System *Client or Demand System* | Organization Output |
|---|---|---|---|---|---|
| | *Social System* | *Technical-Operation System* | | | |
| **Focus of Change** *Individual* | Counseling Coaching Management Train- ing Testing Individual Feedback Personal Develop. Prog. Management Profil- ing Life/Career Planning | Job Rotation Technical Training Performance Review Job Enrichment | Policy-Procedure Analysis and Change —Incentives —Hours —Promotions | Role Requirements and Relationships with Clients | P/L Production Costs Quality Turnover Absenteeism Service |

|  |  |  |  |  | Intermediate Outputs |
|---|---|---|---|---|---|
| *Interpersonal and Team* | Team Building—MBO<br>Team Training<br>RAT (Role Analysis Technique)<br>Data—Feedback<br>Group Diagnosis Instruments<br>Meeting Engineering<br>Process Consultation<br>T-group | Work Flow Analysis<br>Work Re-design<br>Job Enrichment<br>Work Team Formation<br>Job Planning | Goal Setting<br>Policy-Re-examination<br>Motivation and Control System Analysis<br>Scheduling | Open System Planning<br>Open System Mapping | Grievances<br>Complaints<br>Conflict<br>Transfers<br>Job Satisfaction |
| *Inter-Group and Total Organization* | Sensing Meetings<br>Mirroring<br>Inter-group Building<br>Confrontation Conference<br>Survey—Feedback<br>Organization Diagnosis Instruments<br>Third Party Peace-making | Work Systems Analysis<br>System Re-design<br>Capital Equipment Improvement or Development | Long Range Planning<br>Strategic Planning<br>Forecasting<br>Budget Review<br>Analysis of Information Systems | Data Gathering from Demand Systems<br>Interface Meetings with Demand Systems<br>Open System Planning<br>Open System Mapping |  |

## 6. Action Taking

After the plan has been carefully developed, it must be implemented. Success in the change program is often dependent on support through sufficient resources, time, and commitment of key personnel to ensure optimum impact.

## 7. Evaluation of the Action

Too often change programs omit advance determination of how success or failure will be measured; ideally, the plan should be monitored carefully to assess the actual impact of the action on those involved. Evaluation may mean a review of production records for a period of time following the action plan, or it may mean looking at turnover or grievance rates or administering another climate or attitude survey. It is possible that the evaluation will indicate that the problem still exists because the original diagnosis-action planning sequence was faulty or new factors have emerged that require another plan.

The above formulation assumes that creating change is approached in the general problem-solving manner, through which certain general activities and skills can be applied. Central to all problem solving-change actions is appropriate clarification and formulation of the condition that needs to be changed followed by an adequate diagnosis based on data gathered from all relevant sources. Next comes the phase of action most often referred to as the "change strategy." Without an adequate formulation and diagnosis, it is doubtful that an effective change plan can be devised. Developing an action plan may be a creative process, but it should be based on an adequate theory as to how and why people change their behavior. Much of this book will be an exploration of alternative action or change strategies and their connection with behavior change.

# Implications for Managing Change

Before any change strategy is developed, it is critical that the target of change be clearly identified. If the focus of change is an individual, the *specific* change strategy will be different than if the target is a group of interacting individuals or merely a collection of people identified together for some common purpose.

While the specific change plan will vary depending on the target of change, a *general* change program may be appropriate in formulating the overall plan of action. In every case, the problem or condition to be changed must be clearly identified. Data should be gathered regarding the "cause" or emergence of the problem. After these data are analyzed, the *specific* action plan can be developed. If the focus is an individual, the plan must take into account a variety of specific factors relating to that person—attitudes, values, experience, intelligence, idiosyncracies, personal expectations, self-concept, ego strength, etc. When a group or interactive unit is the target and a group outcome (productivity, quality, attendance, morale) is desired, it is necessary to understand the group dynamics operating. Here, the specific change plan would involve group participation, decision making, influence, and support. If a collectivity—the buying public, voters, automobile drivers, homeowners—is seen as the object of change, the usual goal is to alter a rate, such as percent purchasing or voting. The change strategy is geared toward influencing a certain percentage of the collectivity in a desired direction. Usually the change agent is concerned not with individual change but with improvement of the rate.

Effective change programs have built-in evaluation procedures to determine if the plan has in fact achieved its goals.

# CHAPTER 2
# Emergence of Planned Change

The notion that individuals and organizations can become locked into unproductive patterns has a long history. There is the interesting case in Exodus 18 of Moses receiving counsel from his father-in-law, Jethro, who observed that Moses was ineffectively managing the Children of Israel. Jethro, who was probably the first change agent, saw that Moses was overwhelmed from morning until evening handling the disputes and problems of everyone who wanted his services. Jethro had gathered the data, made a diagnosis that this process was not in the best interest of either Moses or his people, and then suggested a plan of action. To increase efficiency, Jethro advised Moses to create an organization with "rulers of thousands, rulers of hundreds, rulers of fifties, rulers of tens" who would conduct everyday business and pass only the toughest cases on to Moses. When Jethro says, "If thou shalt do this thing . . . then thou shalt be able to endure all, and this people shall also go to their place in peace," he clearly identifies the action to be taken and the positive consequences that would result.

This early case encompasses all the elements of planned change. Someone observes a situation in which conditions or consequences are not as positive as could be expected. This observer, who is held in esteem by the key person involved in the problem situation, suggests a course of action. According to the scriptures, Moses behaved in a most remarkable way: "So Moses hearkened to the voice of his father-in-law and did all that he had said" (Exodus 18:24). It is not often that the recommendations of the change agent are accepted so completely, or with such success, by the client. It is difficult to know what "motivated" Moses to follow Jethro's counsel. Was it out of respect for Jethro's authority and position as father-in-law? Was it the power of shared observations and the impact of the data? Was Moses so worn out by the existing pattern he was willing to try anything? Perhaps all of these, and other factors, combined to produce a successful change effort.

# Hawthorne Studies

Shift now to a much later time. The Hawthorne studies, conducted around 1930 by investigators from Harvard at the Western Electric plant in Hawthorne, Illinois, were not planned change programs, but research efforts to determine what forces affected workers' performance. These original pioneering studies showed that changes in worker's performance could not be accurately predicted by altering external stimuli such as lighting, rest periods, or pay. A key factor was how the group of workers felt about the changes and the decisions they commonly agreed to implement. These studies indicated clearly that worker performance could be improved if workers were allowed freedom to control their own work, were treated with respect, and were able to build group support.

# Force-Field Analysis

During World War II, the government of the United States became involved in planned change. At that time, meat was rationed, and scarce ration stamps were required to secure the choice cuts of meats—roasts, steaks, and chops. Other cuts of meat, such as liver, brain, tongue, and heart, were not rationed, but were not being used. Kurt Lewin, a professor at the University of Iowa, was asked to research on whether it was possible to get housewives to change their meat-buying and eating habits and to start using these nonrationed products.

With his research assistants, Lewin set up experimental conditions. Some housewives were put in groups that listened to "attractive lectures . . . which linked the problem of nutrition with the war effort, emphasized the vitamin and mineral value of the [nonrationed] meats. . . . Both the health and economic aspects were stressed. The preparation of these meats was discussed in detail. . . . Mimeographed recipes were distributed" (Lewin, 1958). Yet despite these extensive efforts, only 3 percent of the audience served any of the nonrationed cuts of meats.

Other housewives were asked to participate in discussion groups regarding food, nutrition, the war effort, and what they could do to assist. Following these sessions, it was found that 32 percent of the women served at least one of the previously avoided products. Apparently something that prompted change was present in the group sessions but not in the lectures. Lewin's own analysis indicates he considered the differences were due to (1) the degree of involvement of people in the discussion, (2) the motivation in actually being a party to the decision to use nonrationed meats, and (3) group influence and support in reinforcing the decision.

From this and similar research, Lewin developed a model for analyzing

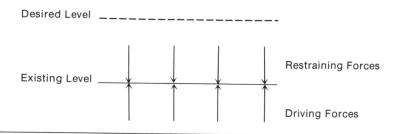

the planned-change process. He visualized the existing condition in a state of balance or equilibrium (with some fluctuation) between two sets of forces—driving and restraining. He called his model of counterbalancing forces "force field analysis." (See Figure 2.1.)

In Lewin's meat-eating problem, the restraining forces that kept housewives from using the nonrationed meats seemed to be taste, smell, appearance, family reactions, low status attached to eating these meats, lack of approval by others, and lack of information about preparation. Driving forces that pushed toward change were patriotism, hunger, nutrition, no stamp requirement, and new experience. Apparently, drive was not enough to overcome the strength of the resistance.

## Change Strategies

The field-of-forces model provides three basic change strategies:

1. *Increase* the driving forces.
2. *Decrease* the restraining forces.
3. Do both.

There is good evidence to suggest that just increasing the driving forces results in a degree of increased resistance, and change may not be maintained unless pressure is constantly applied. According to Lewin, change occurs when the existing situation is "unfrozen," moved to a new level, and then "refrozen" at the new position. Just applying more pressure does not seem adequate to refreeze the change at the new level.

More appropriate is the strategy of reducing or eliminating restraints or, even better, moving previously restraining forces around to the driving side. In the meat-eating case, the lecture attempted to increase pressure—

appealing to patriotism in helping the war effort and trying to reduce the restraint of lack of preparation knowledge by passing out recipes.

The group discussion-decision method changed peer-group pressure from a restraining force to a driving force. Women who formerly had been uneasy about the reactions of their peers were now getting support from those very peers. Yet even the group-process method was not strong enough to overcome certain resistance forces: More than 65 percent of the women still would not use the undesirable cuts of meat.

## Force-Field Analysis and Organization Problem-Solving (Action Research)

It is apparent that the flow of activity in force-field analysis follows the problem-solving steps listed in Chapter 1. However, the force-field model, called "action research," defines a number of actions that are different from the problem-solving sequence. It is advisable to look at both models.

### 1. Define the Problem and Determine the Change Goals

In planned change, one begins with the existing situation, which is seen as a "problem" or a condition to be altered. Lewin's model suggests the same beginning but emphasizes defining clearly the existing condition as well as the desired condition to be achieved.

### 2. Gather the Data

In order to identify the *real* forces in the situation, it is important to gather accurate information about both resistance forces and positive factors. If possible, it is helpful to learn which forces are most critical and which are amenable to change. Some factors may be open to change but are really not important, and some very important forces may be outside the ability of people to influence to any great degree. As indicated earlier, data-gathering may be accomplished by interviews, questionnaires, instruments, or direct observations. However they are acquired, the results are fed back into the system as the basis for achieving change.

### 3. Summarize and Analyze the Data

Accumulated data are put into a summary form. For larger amounts of data, sophisticated computer and statistical analyses may be necessary. For interviews or direct observations, dominant "themes" or issues mentioned by several respondents should be identified. In force-field analyses, the emphasis should be on understanding the complexity of the factors. This includes determining which factors are most important, which are amenable to change, which cannot be influenced or modified, and which have the greatest probability for lending themselves to a successful change endeavor.

## 4. Plan the Action

Following analysis of the data, the plan of action is prepared. In a good action plan, the following matters are considered:

a) Who are the significant people who must support a change program?
b) Where should action-taking begin?
c) Who should be assigned to take what specific action?
d) When should first reports of action be prepared for review?
e) What resources (time, money, equipment, personnel) are needed for the change program?
f) What is the estimated completion time?

## 5. Take Action

After the plan of action has been carefully worked out, the next logical step is to put the plan into effect. Lewin's model would encourage the following in the action-taking stage:

a) Work on reducing restraining forces.
b) Involve people in planning their own change.
c) Develop social supports for change.
d) Get people to make their own decisions to change.

## 6. Evaluate

Any good action research program contains the criteria for its own success. How do you know if you have reached your goals? Goals should be stated in such a way that evaluation criteria are evident and easily applied. For example, if an organization stated its change goal as "improving communications," success would be very difficult to measure. Any increase in talking could be said to "improve communications." A more measurable goal would be: "Have every manager conduct a sharing and evaluation session with each of his subordinates every three months." Measurement of this change goal is possible. If it has not been achieved, the action-research model must be recycled: gathering new data, analyzing it, and repeating the whole process.

## Group Participation—Coch–French Study

One of Lewin's students, J. R. P. French, along with Lester Coch conducted a famous 1948 study that helped establish the use of groups as a vehicle for successful change. Their research concerned getting workers to accept and adapt to changes in the work setting, in a garment-man-

ufacturing plant. The standard method of changing work procedures—
to call workers together and announce the forthcoming change—was
usually accompanied by a great deal of worker resistance, turnover, and
production loss.

   As part of the experiment, a second change method was introduced.
Management met with a group of workers, explained the need for change,
and had the workers select three representatives to try the new procedures
and then help the rest of the workers handle the transition. The result
was that the group reached its previous level of productivity in fourteen
days with no one quitting and only one grievance.

   A third method was to involve everyone affected by the change plan.
After the need for change was explained, the entire group was allowed
to develop its own work procedures to cope with the new conditions.
This method resulted in the fastest relearning. Not only did the workers
return to the previous rate of output, they actually surpassed it by 14
percent within thirty days. There were no resignations, no absenteeism,
and no grievances. This applied research has supported the importance
of universal participation in planned change.


## Change and Anxiety

An important consideration in implementing a change plan is coping with
the resultant anxiety, particularly when the change initially decreases
productivity. Coch and French found that even under the best of change
conditions, production falls off when workers are asked to change assignments and begin new, unfamiliar work. This dropoff in performance
is usually accompanied by an increase in anxiety on the part of those who
began the change program. (See Figure 2.2.)

   At the point of heightened anxiety and decreasing performance, there
is a desire to cancel the whole change effort and return to the earlier state;
bad as it was, it seems better than the new condition. There are times
when a change program is poorly conceived and should be cancelled.
But if the plan is based on data, those involved choose the change, plans
are thought through, and people are committed to them, the major issue
then is to manage the anxiety—not the change. The Coch–French study
found that it takes about two weeks for a turnaround in motor skill
performance to occur. In other areas it may take many months before
improvement is noticeable. People manage their anxiety best by talking
honestly about their concerns, reviewing the progress and the plans, and
making modifications as needed. No one can guarantee the success of
every change program. There always will be elements of risk and surprise
and sometimes failure. One plans for change because action seems a better
course than inaction. If the plan is well conceived, initiated, and carried

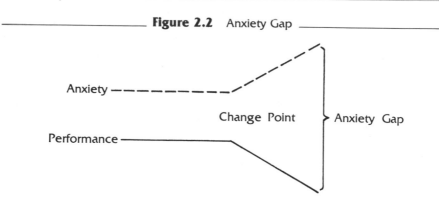

**Figure 2.2**   Anxiety Gap

out, the chances for success seem better than the slow erosion of a deteriorating situation where nothing is done.

## Implications for Managing Change

Helping people change ineffective behaviors goes far back in history. Moses' father-in-law, Jethro, helped Moses see that his existing pattern of administration was ineffective and suggested a new way of organizing and implementing activities. Moses accepted the change plan, and apparently the results were positive.

Modern behavior science has focused on what factors seem to be present when people change their behavior. The Hawthorne studies around 1930 and the work of Lewin and his associates during and following World War II demonstrated the powerful effect of group influences in supporting change. Lewin's work emphasized the importance of general involvement in the change program, reducing resistance factors rather than pushing for change, and giving people social support in the change effort. All of these are important strategy issues.

Behavioral scientists continue to examine the matter of performance change. One example is the work of Latham and others (1981), who developed a three-stage approach for improving employee productivity. Their general strategy, similar to that already described, includes identifying the nature of the poor performance, deciding what causes it, and then coping with the causes. Their specific strategy includes defining the performance in a precise behavioral way, setting performance goals, giving training in new behaviors, and ensuring a reward for improved performance.

In planning change, one important factor that is sometimes disruptive to change agents is timing. Changes does not always, and perhaps does not usually, occur immediately. It may take a period of time to develop the skill to implement a behavioral change or adjust to a new standard or new policy. Sometimes those who initiate change must deal with their own anxiety when performance does not improve as quickly as they would like. They must learn to manage the anxiety, which means allowing time for the change to occur without getting upset too soon and abandoning a change process that might be appropriate and could achieve the desired results if adequate time were allowed.

# CHAPTER 3

# Motivation and
# Planning for Change

Unplanned changes can result from a chance event, a new discovery or invention, a crisis or catastrophe, or the movement or shifting of people. But a planned change is contrived action and occurs when someone decides that a condition or situation is not adequate and should be altered, usually with the goal of improvement.

All planned change involves a strategy to get others to alter their behavior. Certain factors that significantly influence behavior should be considered when one engages in action planning. These forces motivate people to spend time, energy, and resources to bring about a change.

## Felt Need

An important piece of research on behavior change was contributed by Dalton in 1970. After reviewing the literature on change, he identified a number of conditions that seemed to be present when behavior change occurred. In almost every case, he noted a need to change in those who were asked to alter performance. But the person who initiated the change also had to have a "felt need" strong enough to move him or her to take action.

A fundamental issue in planned change is how to create a felt need sufficient to take action. This felt need may be directed towards oneself— for example, managers who, as part of a management development or training program, must develop a need to improve their own performance. The felt need also may be directed towards others to improve conditions in the organization. The change agent or change team basically asks: "How can a need to change be produced in people to get them to increase the output of their department, reduce costs, or improve quality?"

One definition of a "felt need" is a condition of internal disturbance, tension, or imbalance that impels a person to take action to reduce the tension and return to a state of equilibrium or balance. Part of the change strategy is to create this state of tension, imbalance, or felt need. Elements in such strategies are discussed below.

# Disparity Models

Most of the popular theories or models of managerial behavior have a disparity condition built into their formulations. All disparity models are based on the assumption that a change strategy must create a recognition of the difference between what an individual holds as his or her ideal goal, or objective, and what he or she is *actually* doing, thinking, or accomplishing. When a model presents an "ideal" state or style of management performance that either explicitly or implicitly is presented as a goal, persons examining the model cannot help but compare their own state with the ideal. If the actual performance is perceived as less than the ideal, a disparity condition has been created that presumably will inspire improvement. A number of current management theories are reviewed in the table of minimal and maximal conditions (see Table 3.1). These very popular models—Theory X and Y, 9–1 to 9–9, etc.—all display a disparity quality. Presumably, all managers fall somewhere between the high (ideal) and low types and thus will be motivated to improve.

## TABLE 3.1
### Minimum and Maximum Positions
### in Selected Management Theories

| Theorist | Minimum Position | Maximum Position |
|---|---|---|
| Douglas McGregor | *Theory X:* Assumptions that managers hold about people: they dislike work, need coercion, want security, want direction. | *Theory Y:* Assumption of manager that worker likes work, is self-motivated, accepts responsibility. |
| Rensis Likert | *System 1:* Exploitive, authoritative management. High control of people by the manager. | *System 4:* Participative group. Manager allows worker to participate in organizational matters. |
| Robert Blake and Jane Mouton | *1–1 Style:* Low concern for both production or results and people. | *9–9 Style:* Optimum concern for both production, goals, results, and the people who must achieve the results. |
| Abraham Maslow | Management concerned with only physiological or safety needs. | *Eupsychian Management:* Self-actualized managers dealing with self-actualized people. |

Management-development programs based on one or more of the above theories usually attempt, by a variety of methods, to get managers to see themselves at some point between the low and the high positions and then try to move closer to the ideal level.

## How to Create Awareness of Disparity

There are currently several methods used to create an awareness of the disparity between existing and ideal conditions:

### 1. Cognitive Insight

Most literature, lectures, and training films use a disparity orientation to move the reader, hearer, or viewer to engage in personal analysis and change in the preferred direction. It is expected that managers, through their own internal dialogue, will gain insight about themselves and see themselves somewhere below the ideal. It is obvious that merely presenting information cannot ensure that the respondent will see himself or herself accurately; the information may create a disparity that is not consistent with reality. It has often been observed that a key executive reading about a new management tool such as team building, job enrichment, or management by objective (MBO) embarks on an improvement program that may not be what is really needed in the organization. Cognitive insight from the sources listed above is not usually adequate by itself as the basis for a change program.

### 2. Interpersonal Feedback

A second disparity-producing method is to arrange for a person to obtain direct, immediate, accurate, and helpful feedback about his or her management style or organizational performance from those who have interacted with him or her. The open exchange of verbal feedback is commonly regarded as the most personal of the disparity models and the one with the most impact. The assumption is that either the person receiving the feedback is unaware of his or her impact on others, or his or her self-perception is at odds with reality. In either case, feedback should reveal enough disparity to move him or her toward change. Some problems in using feedback are discussed later.

### 3. Surveys or Instruments

There are a number of data-gathering instruments that give a person extensive and sometimes statistically precise data about his or her performance, style, and impact on the performance or attitude of others in the organization. These instruments are circulated to co-workers; the data are then tabulated, summarized, and given to the subject on the assumption that the data will reveal a disparity and inspire change. Surveys are also used to gather organizational data; indications that conditions in the organization are less than optimal may create a need for change.

## 4. Reports

Most reporting systems assume a disparity orientation. If a report shows that performance is down from the previous quarter or is below what was projected, this disparity ideally will create energy for change.

## Problems in Using Disparity Models

There are a number of issues that plague all disparity models, particularly those emphasizing feedback as the method of producing disparity. The more important issues are these:

## 1. Who Reveals the Disparity?

Without feedback, it is difficult to locate oneself in comparison with the ideal. If a person would like to be at System 4 (participative management), from whom does he or she need feedback to get a clear picture of his or her actual performance? Whose feedback will make a difference? One can imagine a manager dismissing data from subordinates or peers he or she does not respect. Or one could be so responsive to feedback from one's boss that all other sources of information are disregarded.

## 2. How Intense Is the Feedback?

Do people respond more to high-intensity feedback, in which issues are strongly stated and the emotional loading is great, or to low-key information conveyed in a more gentle or restrained manner? Do some people respond to high-intensity feedback and others to low-key responses? If so, how do we determine who is to receive what kinds of data? Or do we disregard this factor and give all people the same information? More research is needed regarding these issues; those planning to create disparity via feedback should test the intensity factor carefully.

## 3. How Much Data Should Be Given?

To maximize the possibility that a person will change some aspects of his or her behavior, is it better to convey one piece of information at a time so that he or she does not feel overwhelmed? Or is it better to unload all the data so that he or she can have a total picture of his or her performance and, starting with this "gestalt," do a better job of planning? Are people overwhelmed with too much feedback, or do they simply shrug off sketchy data?

## 4. How Is the Disparity Revealed?

Is it better to create disparity through a one-shot feedback session, or would a series of sessions be better? Is it best done on the job or away from the job in a relaxed setting conducive to introspection and reflection? Is it best done by personal one-to-one verbal feedback or through an instrumented process where data-gathering devices are used and one can review the written data in private?

## 5. When Should Disparity Be Revealed?

Is feedback more powerful if it is given when a person asks for it, or when someone wants to share it? Is it best immediately after an interaction or later, when people have had a chance to think things over? Does feedback early in one's career have more impact than after one has been entrenched in a position for years? What happens if the disparity is created at a time when a person is being reviewed for a raise in salary or a promotion? Timing is an important factor.

Feedback used to create disparity must be managed carefully and the above issues carefully considered. A manager could receive so much feedback from threatening people in such an intense way that the resulting disparity overwhelms him or her and leads to his or her resigning or giving up in despair.

## The Use of Feedback in Creating Disparity

Do the potential problems in using feedback to create a disparity or felt need mean it should not be used? Of course not! But before any feedback program is put into practice, the questions raised above should be carefully considered. There is clear evidence from the study of the use of feedback at General Electric (Meyer, 1972) that feedback that is critical, unclear or imprecise or that comes from powerful people can have negative results. The GE research also showed that performance improved most when feedback was used primarily as a vehicle to identify areas for improvement and when specific plans and goals were set by boss and subordinate.

The use of the Personal Management Interview (PMI) has been shown by Boss (1983) to be effective in improving performance when feedback is connected to planning.

## The Planning Process

Following are the factors in a good planning meeting that appear to support the improvement of performance:

1. *Planning is a joint effort between boss and subordinate.* The GE study demonstrated that results are better when the subordinates are

asked to evaluate their own performance (self-feedback) and their comments become the basis of the superior's feedback. With this common base, plans for improved performance are developed together.

**2.** *The planning is done in an atmosphere of support and trust.* The superior must show by action and communication that he or she is primarily concerned with helping the subordinate. The planning session is not one of punitive confrontation or demands for change but rather of joint determination for improvement.

**3.** *Planning is done on a regular basis.* Too often, performance reviews are scheduled on a yearly or semiyearly basis and are held primarily to allow the superior to give feedback to the subordinate. Effective planning is done regularly (from his research, Boss suggests every two weeks or once a month).

**4.** *Plans are written and copies are shared by boss and subordinate.* The plans state: 1) what is to be done; 2) when the action should be taken; and 3) what help or support should come from the boss.

**5.** *Consequences are reviewed regularly.* Each planning session includes a review of the consequences of the previous plan for which the superior must be willing to hold the subordinate accountable. If performance did not improve, the superior must ask why and stress the subordinate's responsibility for implementing agreements.

## Dissonance Reduction

Disparity also can be seen as the creation of dissonance in a person. Cognitive dissonance, which has received a good deal of attention in behavioral science research (Festinger, et al., 1956), occurs when one's belief is shown to be at odds with reality. Examples of cognitive dissonance include the conviction that the world is coming to an end, when in fact it is not, as well as more commonplace experiences such as believing that one cannot afford a new car but buying a new Super Charger Eight anyway. When a disparity or dissonance is established, there is "motivation" to reduce the dissonance.

According to dissonance reduction theory, common reactions include 1) denying one's previously held beliefs or altering them to conform to reality; or 2) holding to the beliefs but building a set of rationalizations as to why reality is really not at odds with the belief system. Evidence indicates that those who buy new cars they cannot afford will read more articles stating that new cars are more economical, the price will increase more next year, and there will be fewer repair bills. They will convince themselves that their purchase was wise.

In a change strategy, one way to create motivation is to fashion a disparity between what is and what people believe. If workers who believe they are productive are given data that show they are not really as productive as they thought, a motivation set might be established that will push them to change. But the dissonance reduction model points out the pitfalls in such a strategy. It is possible that the workers will accept the data, drop the belief that they are productive, and try to produce more to reestablish their image. However, it is also possible that they could hold to their belief and rationalize that the data about productivity are wrong. If they decide they are as productive as conditions allow and that management wants to exploit them, they will become more entrenched in their belief system. It has been demonstrated that if people are involved in gathering their own data, they are less likely to create rationalizations than if others tell them the facts.

## Implications for Managing Change

All this is to say that risk characterizes most change strategies that try to motivate people by creating a disparity between what is and what 'ought' to be. Change agents or change teams should recognize that risk, and plan strategies that reduce the dangers of a boomerang effect. This seems to be best accomplished by making clear, accurate data available and having workers participate in the data-gathering and analysis process and help in planning actions that will lead to the desired goals.

Feedback has been one of the major methods of creating disparity—letting people or organizational units know how they are doing and that they are not fulfilling expectations. Although feedback may create a positive motivational disparity, the disparity may be too traumatic or overwhelming, or too biased or limited; thus, the results may not be what the change agent had hoped. Feedback that is clear, precise, and timely and that is used as the basis of joint planning between boss and subordinates seems to have the greatest potential for producing performance change.

# CHAPTER 4
# The Relationship for Helping Change

According to most people, working effectively with others requires first "building a good relationship" or, in other words, "developing rapport," "establishing a good climate," or gaining their confidence." Unfortunately, most discussions stop at this point, as though the subject were covered once the principle is stated. Each person is left to his or her own devices as to how to establish the critical base of the subsequent working relationship. Yet central to the task of any change agent is coexisting with others in ways that will allow work to be accomplished and changes achieved.

A useful framework for building a "good" relationship is to see the change agent and the client as an interactive system in which each has needs, goals, values, and expectations that the other must understand and accommodate.

## Needs

When a potential change agent contacts another person, he or she should keep in mind that this other person represents a collection of needs or conditions that demand satisfaction; if satisfaction is not likely, adjustments must be made. Likewise, the change agent has certain needs that require attention. Although there has been no definitive cataloging of a needs system, one useful model was developed in 1943 by Maslow, who observed a hierarchy of human needs, with each need in the hierarchy dependent on those below it in the system. Certainly in the change agent-client relationship, it is important that each feel some satisfaction of ego needs, some social acceptance, and the potential for achieving something worthwhile.

Each person has a collection of personal needs. Therefore, it would seem apparent that someone who might not meet his or her needs or who might even violate them would not build the same type of relationship as another person who might meet them. Too often, in the interest of getting the job done, managers concentrate on the task and don't take into account the needs of the workers. The change agent can facilitate a relationship by identifying his or her needs in working with the client and asking for similar honesty.

## Values

Each person has not only a complex system of needs, but also a system of values: feelings about certain ideas, concepts, situations, or activities that represent points of concern, of worth, and of importance. Individual value systems vary, and what is valuable to one person may not be valuable to another. For example, a client might value his privacy and his right to make his own decisions; he could value the opinion of a certain newspaper columnist and the efficacy of prayer as a means to answer questions. A change agent who does not know or try to understand the client's value system may engage in activities, make remarks, or suggest actions that are in direct opposition to what the client holds to be of value. Should this occur, the relationship would probably not be characterized by rapport or confidence; rather, it would be strained, antagonistic, uncooperative, and perhaps even hostile. Just as with human needs, anyone desiring to build a good relationship would find it advantageous to understand the other person's value system and to respect it in the course of the interaction. If the change agent has important values that may affect the relationship with the client, he or she should identify them early on. For example, if the change agent highly values participative decision making, the client must understand this aspect of the change agent's views.

## Expectations

Another complex of attitudes crucial to the building of an effective helping relationship consists of the expectations the client and the change agent have regarding each other.

Expectations are feelings that another person should behave in certain ways. Sometimes, when expectations are shared and mutually satisfied, each person knows what others expect of him or her, the result is cohesion and harmony as people meet each others' expectations and consequently reward each other. When expectations are not met, negative reactions, conflict, and disharmony often result. Therefore, negative reactions can occur and the basic relationship is not one of rapport, cohesion, or confidence.

It sometimes happens that someone will consciously and deliberately violate or fail to meet the expectations of another, but this is an unusual occurrence. It is more likely that such a failure results from a lack of information. To ensure satisfaction of expectations, the change agent and the client should spend some time sharing those expectations that are relevant to their work together.

# Goals

As the change agent and client work together, they should have some common understanding of the goals each is trying to achieve. Serious problems occur when the client is working toward one set of objectives and the change agent is going in a different direction; for example, the client might desire greater productivity while the change agent aims at conflict reduction. They also should explore means for achieving the goals. They both might agree on the goal of increased production but disagree as to the means to achieve the goal.

# The Change Agent's Behavior in the Relationship

Basic to successful functioning with respect to a client's needs, values, goals, and expectations is understanding what these are. Some guidelines for gaining this understanding follow.

## Leveling

In opening the interaction with the client, the change agent may announce the desire that each participant "level" with the other. The point is to establish a basic ground rule fundamental to the whole relationship— namely, frankness and honesty.

If the client indicates a willingness to adopt such a ground rule, the change agent may wish to ask the members of the client system to let him or her know honestly how they feel concerning their needs, values, and expectations. He or she might ask for information such as the following:

1. When is it most convenient for me to come and work with you? (What are your expectations about time arrangements?)
2. What do you think I ought to do when I work with you?
3. Do you have any apprehensions or feelings of anxiety about having me come?
4. How do you feel about conditions in your system?
5. What bothers you most about your situation in this system?

## Sharing

An important part of the leveling process is the reciprocal sharing of data between the change agent and the client. A good working relationship is based on mutual understanding and shared confidence. It is as important for the change agent to share with the client as vice versa. The change agent is at something of a disadvantage in sharing ideas, information, and feelings insofar as his or her professional role may limit the amount of data he or she can share. However, the change agent may talk with the system members about such things as:

1. What I consider my role in working with you.
2. What I think a good change agent-client relationship should be.
3. Some of the anxieties I have in performing my work.
4. What I see as some of my competencies in working with you.

The keynote is that both the change agent and the client *begin* their experience by talking about the relationship. Although the ultimate concern is the achievement of system objectives, a strong relationship must be built in order to work effectively on the problems.

## Individual Differences

It is a cliché that "all people are different," but it nevertheless is important to keep this fact in mind. The individual mix of needs, values, goals, and expectations is different for every person. Because no one approach applies to every situation, the change agent must develop or increase his or her sensitivity, which has been defined as the ability to discriminate clearly among individuals on the basis of their characteristics. Some persons are capable of seeing individual differences more accurately than others and thus are able to respond more appropriately. It has been said that "The more successful supervisor may be the one best able to perceive these individual characteristics in order to tailor his or her own actions to the individual's unique qualities."

The ability to differentiate between individuals and to respond appropriately to their differences is an important aspect of the change agent-client relationship; increasing this ability would be valuable training for persons who must work closely with others. Those who are rather rigid and inflexible in their responses to others may have difficulty in making the appropriate modifications for individual differences. Perhaps inflexibility, if it cannot be modified, should be considered negatively in the selection of change agents whose jobs put them in contact with many different people. There is certainly evidence that sensitivity and flexibility are vital to good interpersonal relations. The question now is *how* to increase these qualities in the change agent.

# The Communication of Acceptance

From the fields of counseling and therapy comes the notion of interpersonal acceptance. This involves the subtle communication from one person to another of genuine interest and concern and, more important, willingness to try to understand the other person without evaluation and judgment.

Feelings of nonacceptance can be communicated in many ways, both verbally and nonverbally. Some people working in homes of those in a social class lower than their own experience a sense of revulsion toward people living in conditions so unlike what they are used to. If they were to react negatively to the "unsanitary" surroundings, implying their own feelings of superiority, they would establish an atmosphere of nonacceptance.

# Nonacceptance and Acceptance

What are the behaviors that tend to make a person feel accepted or nonaccepted? Table 4.1 may help identify behavioral inputs that result in feelings of acceptance or nonacceptance.

---

### TABLE 4.1
### Behavioral Inputs

#### Acceptance

- Listening
- Accepting one's ideas
- Sharing information
- Genuine interest in the other person
- Expressions of appreciation

#### Nonacceptance

- Criticisms
- Unfair comparisons
- Avoidance
- Advice-giving
- Rejection of one's ideas
- Laughing at, not with
- Pretending to listen
- All pretending behavior (pretending to be interested, concerned, etc.)

---

What are the results of the nonaccepting relationship? It's predictable that if a member of the client's system did not feel acceptance from the change agent, some of the following things might occur:

## 1. *Results of nonacceptance*

    *a.* Antagonistic feelings

    *b.* Noncooperation

    *c.* Avoidance of the change agent

    *d.* Minimal sharing of information

    *e.* Noncompliance with suggestions or advice

    *f.* Feelings of relief when the relationship is terminated

All the above are conditions that would plague the change agent and prevent him or her from accomplishing his or her goals with the system. On the other hand, if the change agent were able to develop the kind of accepting relationship discussed here, we could predict more of the following:

## 2. *Results of acceptance*

    *a.* Sharing of information

    *b.* Cooperation

    *c.* Feelings of closeness

    *d.* Willingness to work interdependently

    *e.* Positive anticipation of the change agent's return

# Problems in Developing a Helping Relationship

As indicated above, the behavioral inputs from the change agent to people in the system influence feelings of acceptance or nonacceptance. But it is difficult for the change agent to get a clear picture of how his or her behavior is being experienced by the system members he or she is trying to help. If the change agent thinks his or her behavior is appropriate, he or she will continue to behave in the same way until discovering that it is not. Some ways of checking one's behavioral inputs include:

1. An evaluation questionnaire circulated to the system members.
2. Periodic interviews by supervisors or an outside person to monitor the reaction of system members.
3. A visit to the system by an observer who could watch the change agent in action. (Following this, an honest exchange of information would be given.)
4. Tape-recording a visit, with subsequent critique by a group of colleagues. It is important to get an honest evaluation of performance as the work with others progresses.)

It is apparent that building an effective relationship involves not only information about what is needed but also skills in working with others and attitudes appropriate to the goal. In this respect, training in building effective relationships with others requires a concentration on information, skills, and attitudes. Too much current training emphasizes primarily the acquiring of information.

## Implications for Managing Change

Fundamental to the change agent's successful interactions is the building of a relationship conducive to work. If the interaction is in constant turmoil because of feelings of mistrust, nonacceptance, suspicion, and defensiveness, the energies of both the change agent and the client are being dissipated nonproductively rather than being directed toward results. The ability to be sensitive to the feelings and attitudes of another person and to respond without compromising one's own position is an important skill that change agents should learn and improve.

The change agent may be learning to change while trying to create change. To be effective, the change agent may need to improve his or her own ability to establish relationships while implementing the change goals of the client. In such cases it is essential for the change agent to get clear feedback from the client as to their basic working relationship. In improving the relationship, the change agent has an opportunity to be a role model for the client by demonstrating how a change relationship is actually achieved.

# CHAPTER 5
# The Ethics of Change

Currently, the change agent role has not yet evolved into a profession with an accepted set of ethical standards and a licensing procedure for consultants. This may come in the future, but until that time those who engage in creating change—the parent, teacher, or manager, as well as the full-time consultant or organization-development specialist—will have to wrestle with certain ethical considerations. Their actions are not illegal or a violation of a moral code. Still, people who are affected by change plans have strong feelings about what is appropriate or "right." When change agents do not understand their feelings and do not work out appropriate agreements, change programs can be put in jeopardy.

## The Use of Data or Information

Since almost every change program involves some data-collection—either through face-to-face interviews or some type of questionnaire—the change agent usually faces issues regarding the use of data. The major concerns are: 1) How much anonymity is expected and how much can be assured? 2) Is it ever appropriate to violate information given in confidence? 3) Can one guarantee how the data will or will not be used?

*1. Anonymity.* Whenever one gathers data, the question inevitably arises of how much of this information, in what form, can be shared with others. The change agent and the informant should agree in advance about this issue. The change agent could tell the informant initially, "Anything you tell me I will want to be able to share with others. Don't tell me anything you do not want repeated." Such an agreement frees the change agent from wondering what to share and what to keep private but may seriously restrict the information the respondent may be willing to share.

A different approach is to say, "Please tell me when you want information off-the-record. I will not share any data specified as confidential." This approach may give the change agent access to critical data that the informant may not want discussed. The informant also may not want to be identified as the source of the information. This last point is important: Does the respondent want certain information withheld, or only to remain unconnected with the data? If it is the latter, the respondent may be willing to have his or her response tabulated if no one knows what he or she said specifically. If the change agent has data that the informant does not want shared, the change agent is seriously restricted. And what happens if the change agent is asked by one informant to keep certain information off-the-record but other informants want the issue presented openly?

If a self-administered anonymous questionnaire is used, some respondents would consider it a violation of privacy if others saw their handwriting, or if their comments were to be shared verbatim, even if no names were attached, for fear that they would be connected with certain terms or phrases.

**2.** *Obligation.* Are there times when the change agent has a moral obligation to reveal confidential data? Most counselors or therapists periodically face the issue of what to do when a client shares information about plans that are self-destructive or harmful to others. Often, they tell the client openly that any data that the counselor deems potentially harmful will *not* be held in confidence. Does the organizational change agent adopt the same stance? A change agent hired to help reduce conflict in the labor force may learn in confidence in the course of gathering data that some workers are planning to sabotage key equipment or to slow down production deliberately so management cannot meet important shipments. What does the change agent do with such information? Given such issues, it is apparent why some change agents declare initially that "all data will be shared. Don't tell me anything you don't want shared with others."

**3.** *Assurances.* People who share information often want assurances. Sometimes they ask, "Will top management see the results of these interviews and will they use the data to make some needed changes?" An agreement as to the *disposition of the data* should be made with the client at the outset. Most change agents would want to assure every respondent that appropriate people would see the data and that a summary of the data would be shared with all respondents. It generally would not be appropriate to promise that specific changes would result from the data. Although no one can predict exactly how the data might be used and what kind of results will occur, the change agent could promise that the data will be reviewed and the reactions of management will be shared with those who provided the data.

Sometimes, as part of a management training program, data about a manager's performance are collected and shared. Participants have a right to be assured that no data gathered for training purposes will be passed on to management for evaluation purposes. It would almost destroy a management development program if confidential information given to the participant from his or her boss, peers, or subordinates was used in performance evaluation. There are legitimate ways through some assessment procedures to observe a participant in a training setting and to gauge the participant's potential.

## Evaluations

Almost every change agent working with an organization has been asked by different members of the client system, "Tell us how you see us (our organization, or Department X or Manager Y). You have been observing us for some time and we would like to know the results of your observations." It should be made clear in advance what kinds of data summaries, impressions, and evaluations the change agent will make. Most people who work with a change agent would consider it unethical if the change agent's impressions or evaluations were passed on to their supervisors without their knowledge or agreement.

**CASE.** The consultant who had just completed a management training program for twenty-four managers of the Heritage Realty Company was having a critique session with the company president, who was also the founder and owner. The consultant, as per the agreement, reviewed the strengths and weaknesses of the program as he saw them.

The president then asked, "Tell me whom you saw as the most capable managers in the program and whom as the poorest." The consultant replied, politely but firmly, that evaluations of the participants were confidential; under no circumstances would he share that information. The president, visibly upset, threatened never to use the consultant again unless he was given the information he wanted. The consultant, who was very clear about his stand, indicated he would not change his position regardless of the consequences.

Probably the strongest ethical feelings are concerned with sharing evaluations of individuals and, secondly, about sharing negative evaluations of a department or work unit without its knowledge. Sharing reactions to the total organization may be unwise but probably would result in fewer feelings that an ethical standard had been violated.

## Using the Change Agent's Prestige

The outside change agent periodically may find himself or herself in the uneasy position of being used by people inside the organization as a leverage to achieve a desirable decision. If the outside agent has prestige or stature as an "expert," a person in the organization may say to key decisionmakers, "Dr. Blank is in favor of this project and has agreed to work with us. We feel her participation should insure success, and we would like to receive formal approval to go ahead."

One variation of this maneuver is recruiting the outside person to "explain" to upper management what the proposed program is about. Another is to ask the consultant to present the summary of data and recommendations to key management under the assumption that the consultant's prestige will be a positive influencing factor.

The reason such exploitation of the change agent creates "unease" is that at times such requests are legitimate, but at other times they are strategies for manipulation of the decision-making process. Decision-makers in turn may feel it is unethical for a consultant to allow himself or herself to be used to put pressures on them.

## Manipulation

As used here, manipulation refers to those situations in which complete data, although available, are not shared with those who must act on it. A person feels manipulated upon learning after a decision has been made that certain information was withheld. Had that information been made available, a different decision might have resulted.

Change agents can be both the instigators of manipulation and the objects of it. If a change agent decides not to share certain data with the client because it would be unfavorable to the program he or she prefers, the change agent is manipulating the client. If the client deliberately does not reveal all relevant information, then the client is manipulating the change agent.

The ethics of the change agent would seem to require that he or she not engage in manipulative practices and to expect that the client will share *all* relevant data and not attempt to manipulate the change agent. There should be an agreement between change agent and client that any attempts at manipulation by either party would be cause for terminating the relationship.

## The "Right" to Change Anyone's Behavior

Probably the most fundamental of all ethical questions is, "Does anyone have the right to try to change the behavior of another person?" There are two polar positions. On the negative side, some consider planned change to be exploitation. They argue that a management that deliberately engages in strategies to increase production and/or profits is exploiting the workers, particularly if the workers do not share in increased profits. Certain students in this field have felt that management has an unfair (unethical) advantage over workers because it can hire expensive consultants and change agents to assist with their goals.

On the other side, some maintain that as long as there is a "contract," either formal or implicit, stating that the company has a right to expect a "fair day's work for a fair day's pay," management has the right to engage in activities to ensure the fair day's work.

From a purely ethical perspective, should change agents allow themselves to be hired by management to increase management's benefits?

Those who have wrestled with this issue have generally agreed that the change agent is operating on ethical ground in trying to create change as long as the following conditions exist (adapted from Bennis, Benne, & Chin, 1969):

   *a.* The client, including all those affected by the change, voluntarily agrees to participate in the change efforts. This means the client understands the change program clearly and accepts participation in it.
   *b.* The change effort will include a sharing of all relevant data so everyone knows upon what information decisions are being made.
   *c.* Both the client and the change agent agree that either has the right to terminate the relationship at any time if either feels the other is not functioning as agreed or expected, or that the change program is not being conducted appropriately.

There are those who consider this a spurious argument, because people can choose *not* to change their behavior if they feel they are being treated unethically, unfairly, or against their best interests. Others feel that stating the ethical concerns and meeting the basic ethical conditions are critical in beginning a change program with any hope for success.

## Implications for Managing Change

Creating change is a very sensitive issue. Some have asked, "Why does anyone have a right to try and change the behavior of someone else?" The easiest way to avoid being seen as a manipulator is to involve those who must change in the decisions to change and to give them all data concerning why the change is needed.

It is not always feasible or practical to involve everyone affected by the change in the change decisions. How does AT&T involve one million employees in a court decision to spin off its subsidiary companies? The best that can be done is to share all the data with all the employees and ask for their help in implementing the required change.

Every change agent—that is, any person trying to impact someone else in a change direction—should be sensitive to ethical considerations. A lack of responsiveness to matters of confidentiality, anonymity, agreement, and sharing information could seriously damage the change effort, the reputation of the change agent, and the possibility of any change in the future.

# SECTION TWO

# Individual and Interpersonal Change

## Introduction

At times the focus of change is a particular individual. Every manager at some time or other has had a "problem employee." At times one can see even in the best of people certain behaviors that reduce their effectiveness, whereupon one wonders how to help another person change or improve. The helping process goes on all around us. One need not be a professional counselor or therapist to engage in actions designed to assist someone else. In fact, it is when nobody is concerned or tries to intervene in a helpful way that a person needing help must resort to a professional for assistance.

Sometimes the condition one wishes to improve is a relationship between people who must work together. In the family, it can be a parent-child interaction that always seems to end in conflict or hurt feelings. Disruptive interactions go on within all kinds of systems and organizations. This section deals with making a more sophisticated diagnosis of why some people have problems with others and employing actions that can be useful in bringing about improvement in performance.

# CHAPTER 6
# Developing Interpersonal Competency

At the individual level, some people have difficulty in interacting with others in ways that produce desired consequences. The change agent may need to be more effective with the client or may consider that some individuals must improve in the interpersonal area in order to help solve organizational problems. The target of change would be to help the person (a manager, subordinate, or even the change agent) become more competent in his or her relationship with others.

The goal in human interaction is to achieve our intentions. Interpersonal behavior usually begins with one person's initiation of action toward one or more others to achieve some purpose or goal. For example, a manager may call in an employee to clarify a report or to give instructions; later, he may want to instruct, stimulate, encourage, or support the same employee. One way of defining competency in human relations is the ability to translate intentions into desired impact. A change agent or manager who cannot consistently achieve desired impacts may need to engage in some behavior change.

## Intention and Impact

Intentions are the end results or goals we hope to achieve with others as we begin an interaction. Person A has some *intentions* toward B. She wants to encourage, clarify, instruct, or take some action that will be the first step toward achieving this goal. With luck, she will make on B an impact consistent with her intentions.

### Behavioral Gap

Between *intention* and *impact* (which is the actual effect of one's behavior), however, are two major gaps that must be considered and to some degree managed (see Figure 6.1, a diagram of the interpersonal flow). One must translate his or her intentions into behavior, which for some people most of the time, and others some of the time, is a major difficulty. The behavior that is expressed may be a very clumsy representation of the intention.

A talk with the subordinates of a certain manager would reveal that they feel hostile or defensive toward, and resistant to, their boss. A conversation with the boss would disclose that he or she is distressed that the workers feel that way, for he or she certainly did not intend to cause that reaction.

Sometimes we display unconscious intentions that we do not admit even to ourselves because they are socially or personally undesirable. We actually want to achieve certain results, even though we would deny the existence of our intentions. For example, a manager who at some deep level distrusts his or her subordinates can communicate this distrust very accurately through his or her behavior. At the conscious level, he or she would say that the communication of distrust is not the real intention; at the unconscious level, however, the issue of distrust is a serious concern, and the behavior reflects more of the unconscious intention than the manager may be aware. One of the important purposes of feedback is to

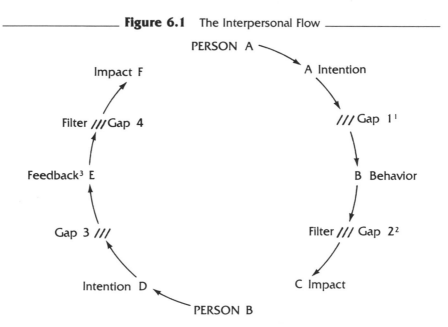

**Figure 6.1**   The Interpersonal Flow

1. Gap 1 is the difference between one's intentions and the behavior that represents them.
2. Gap 2 is the difference between one person's behavior and the other person's perception of it.
3. Feedback is finding out how our behavior has been received by others.

help the receiver honestly examine his or her total intention system, both conscious and unconscious.

## "Filter" System

The distortion between intention and impact also may be in the eye of the beholder. The behavior of A may be a very clear representation of his or her intentions, but if B has a clogged filter system or perceptual screen and perceives the behavior quite differently than was intended, the resulting impact will not be what A desired. All of us have filters; we are aware of some of them and are blind to others. Our filters are composed of our biases, prejudices, values, experiences, and feelings. Person B may have a thick antiauthority filter, which causes him or her to resent anything a superior does. This person interprets attempts to clarify or encourage as disapproval or control. When the boss, with the intention to clarify, interacts with this person, the end result is negative because of how the boss's behavior was interpreted.

In either event, whether the problem of the undesirable impact results from the behavioral gap or filter system, the result for A is the same: he or she has not achieved the consequence intended. As the interaction continues, Person B, who is the object of its interaction, now responds to Person A. B translates his or her intentions into behavior that must pass through A's filter system. Given the possible gaps in the system, it is a wonder that anyone ever gets along with anyone else.

## Competency in Change

Anyone concerned with influencing others to make changes in their performance or behavior must take into account the impact he or she is having on others, particularly those asked to make a change. Whether the person is a manager or professional change agent, one's competency is measured by the degree to which he or she is capable of achieving the intended results. In this framework, the competent person is one who is capable of consistently succeeding.

If he or she wants issues clarified, they become clarified. Should he or she desire to encourage or motivate others, they feel encouraged or motivated following the interaction.

On the other hand, the incompetent person in this model is one who consistently finds that the impact on others is not what was intended. For some reason, this person is plagued by unintended and unanticipated consequences. People are resistant, overly dependent, apathetic, hostile, fearful, frustrated, or cautious when he or she would prefer them to be open, innovative, collaborative, and enthusiastic. Something is going on between the intention and the impact that requires modification or adjustment.

# Influences on Behavior

Soon after one establishes an intention regarding a particular situation, one begins to implement it. Some people will carefully think through their strategies for achieving their intentions and devise a well-crafted plan. Others will move quickly into action, relying on their previous experience, intuition, or best guess. What are the factors that influence behavior as one tries to implement one's intentions? The most crucial factors are style, strategy, and one's definition of the situation.

## Leadership Style

*Style* refers to the rather unconscious habitual pattern of behavior that characterizes a person's performance. One person's leadership style might be described as aggressively autocratic, another's as benevolently autocratic, and still another's as passively introverted or reflectively contemplative.

Fred Fiedler, one of the major researchers in the area of management and leadership, describes leadership style as "the underlying need-structure of the individual which motivates his or her behavior in various leadership situations. Leadership style thus refers to the consistency of goals or needs over different situations" (1967, p. 36).

One's style is such a constant feature of one's behavior that it is difficult to change. It is probably neither possible nor desirable to try to change a person with a quiet, easygoing style into an aggressive, dominant person. The research data are clear on management and leadership effectiveness—people with wide variations in style have been and are successful in their positions. There is evidence that those with certain styles may have a greater chance of success in some situations than in others. A good match between one's style and the demands of the situation is highly desirable. Fiedler found in his research that a person with high needs for structure would be successful in leading a structured task but would be a failure in trying to lead a group in a highly ambiguous task.

There are aspects of personal style, however, that one could change if one were aware of a problem and were willing to work on the issues. For example, a quick temper is a style issue. A person could learn to manage his or her temper and reduce the problems that occur.

## Strategy

While style may be consistent and difficult to change, a person's *strategy* or plan of action can be improved significantly. If one intends an improvement in the performance of others, one can plan a strategy of involvement (having people participate in the improvement program) or devise a threat strategy (threatening punishment or loss of reward if they don't improve). People with quite different styles can implement similar strategies; a quiet person can use threat as well as a loud, aggressive one. But it is apparent that there is some connection between style and strategy, for a manager with an autocratic style may find it harder to engage in a participative strategy.

Different strategies of leadership behavior can be learned. Fiedler (1967), who refers to leadership behavior in the same sense that we discuss strategy, says, "By leadership behavior we generally mean the particular acts in which a leader engages in the course of directing and coordinating the work of his group members. This may involve such acts as structuring the work relations, praising or criticizing group members, and showing consideration for their welfare and feelings." If one ascertains that a strategy is not working—that is, not getting the impact or results intended—one clearly can make an alteration. A manager who finds that being demanding and hardnosed is ineffective may shift to a more supportive strategy.

A major obstacle to translating one's intention into an effective strategy and thus achieving the desired impact is the lack of feedback as to actual results. Subordinates often mask their real reactions to the behavior of the manager and pretend to support decisions or actions when in reality they feel negative and resistant. The more power, status, and influence a person gains, the more reluctant subordinates become to share honest feedback.

## Definition of the Situation

A third factor that affects behavior is the way one defines one's situation. If the manager defines a situation with a subordinate as a crisis requiring immediate action but the subordinate does not see a crisis, the manager will engage in behavior that is considered demanding. The subordinate, whose filter system is not geared to view the situation as a crisis, probably will react negatively to the boss's attempt to pressure him.

Situations can change. If the manager is not aware of the changes, he or she might continue to behave under assumptions that are outdated and inappropriate. One old-line manager had always treated women workers as "the girls" and expected a submissive response to his orders. But the newer women employees who did not appreciate his condescending attitude responded negatively to behavior that never produced such reactions in the past. The situation had changed, but the manager had not seen it.

To ensure a correct definition of the situation, it is often wise to spend time gathering data before one devises a strategy of action.

# Unacted Intentions

It should be obvious that one cannot achieve desired impacts unless action is taken. There are people whose behavior does not appropriately reflect their intentions because of their lack of skill, their inexperience, or their ignorance about useful strategies. There also are people who are afraid to take action and sit silently on their intentions—wishing that something could be done and spinning fantasies of the great accomplishments that might be, but, in the final analysis, doing nothing. In a real sense, inaction is a strategy; it is one way of coping with a situation, and it certainly will have an impact on others. It may not be the impact that one desires, however, so if one intends to be effective as a manager or change agent, he or she will need to plan a more appropriate strategy to achieve the desired impact in a particular situation.

# Implications for Managing Change

It is impossible for anyone to be so all-wise, sensitive, and skillful that he or she always will know exactly the right things to do to produce the desired impacts or results. But it may be possible to develop a strategy that will help devise a further strategy to achieve the desired consequences. Following is an outline of how a manager or change agent might develop an effective interpersonal strategy in collaboration with those he or she wants to influence.

## Declare Intentions

Instead of moving directly into the implementation of intentions, a different approach would be for the manager to talk to the people he or she is trying to influence about what he or she would like to achieve. As a result of this discussion, they would have a clear understanding of his or her intentions rather than guesses based on interpretations of the manager's behavior. If subordinates have not previously experienced such a discussion of intentions, their filter systems may cause them to regard this action with suspicion—as a "gimmick" or trick. The leader must be completely candid in declaring these intentions clearly and then inviting the next step.

## Get Suggestions for Action

The strategy to build a strategy specifies that people next be asked for their ideas, suggestions, and insights about how to achieve the desired results. If a manager's intentions are to motivate the subordinates to greater productivity, he or she might bring them together and honestly announce his or her intentions, what is desired, and why he or she desires it. The manager may find through that process that subordinates' view of the situation is quite different from his or her own and as a result revise his or her intentions. But if the subordinates accept the manager's intentions as valid, they would then offer their suggestions about how to motivate them to increase their production.

## Gathering Feedback

It is critical for anyone wishing to improve his or her ability to achieve impacts consistent with intentions to learn exactly what his or her impact has been on others. This process of finding out one's impact is called *eliciting feedback*. In the absence of feedback, one is in danger of continuing indefinitely an ineffective behavior because one would never know whether or not one were achieving desired impacts.

Although feedback is discussed in more depth in a later chapter, it is necessary to present some of the relevant issues here. Most people have several ways of determining how they affect others. We can get feedback by observation—looking at nonverbal and behavioral cues. Unfortunately, some people cannot accurately see or are unable to interpret this type of signal. Reports are a feedback source. It is also possible to gather feedback directly through a verbal exchange or written responses. Whatever its origin, feedback is needed either to confirm the appropriateness of our actions or to let us know that some change is needed.

The return part of the interpersonal flow is also diagrammed in Figure 6.1. When Person B plans to give Person A feedback about his or her impact, B has intentions about what he or she wants to accomplish. He or she must develop a feedback strategy that will get through Person A's filter system so that A hears the feedback B intended to give. All of this indicates that the improvement of interpersonal behavior is a complex process that requires insight, skill, and a willingness to stay in the relationship and work through the issues with those involved.

# CHAPTER 7
# Eliciting Feedback

The previous chapter identified the use of feedback as part of a change strategy. This chapter addresses how to obtain the clear, accurate data about the impact of our behavior that is such an important part of improving performance.

In current organizational life, people have learned to mask, hide, and cover up their feelings, particularly toward people in positions of power and influence. Because of this, it is often difficult to know what one's true impact on others has been. One may see only the polite smile, the ready agreement, and the apparent consensus and assume, falsely, that these external feedback cues represent the truth.

The person with good interpersonal skills has ways of checking the data to determine his or her actual impact and to ascertain whether the problem, if any, derives from an inability to communicate accurately conscious intentions or lies in the filter systems of others.

In the process of improving one's performance, probably no skill is more important than the ability to gather accurate and honest feedback about one's impact on others. This requires sensitivity, because most people feel fearful and inept confronting someone directly with their feelings about his or her performance. It is not easy for a person in a lower-status position in an organization to face a more powerful, higher-status person with feedback that is unsolicited and presumably unwanted. The risks involved, from the lower-status person's perspective, are so great that unless the situation becomes intolerable, the safest course is to remain silent and hope the passing of time will improve conditions.

This silent minimal-change strategy, widely used for coping with those who have negative impacts on us, masks the real conditions and keeps frustration underground. But until the truth surfaces, the negative consequences of a poor relationship are difficult to manage. The role of the change agent or change team sometimes may be to persuade members of the client system to gather feedback data.

# Techniques for Eliciting Feedback

By creating a climate where others feel safe or even rewarded for sharing information, one is more likely to receive sensitive feedback. How does one go about doing this?

## Individual Direct Request About Specific Areas

Probably the simplest method is to invite the subject to a private one-to-one session. Ideally, this would be preceded by a written memo or verbal request stating the purpose of the meeting, thus giving the person time to prepare. *Example:* "Dear Ed, I would like very much to get your reactions to my management performance. Do you see anything I do that creates problems for others? Do you have any suggestions as to how I might improve my effectiveness? Specifically, I would like your ideas about how I could improve our performance appraisal sessions, our method of giving out assignments, and our procedures for setting goals. I'd like to get together with you next week to talk about it. I'll have my secretary call and set up a time when I can come to your office for a discussion. Thanks, Don."

Many managers indicate that they would appreciate their boss's coming to their offices for such a discussion. Others feel it would not be inappropriate to discuss the matter in the boss's office at a regular discussion meeting. People can prepare for such a session best if they know the specific issues and areas on the agenda.

## Written Feedback

A second method is to request (either verbally or by memo) that the subject write down his or her feelings about specific matters. *Example:* "Ed, I'm trying to improve my own management effectiveness. Would you be willing to take the time to write down any suggestions you have, particularly in the areas of performance review, assignment-giving, and goal-setting? Try to be as honest as possible. I feel it's important to determine my impact on others, both positive and negative."

In a direct request for either verbal or written feedback, the person asked may feel put on the spot. If one's boss is making the request, one may feel obligated to cooperate but uneasy because of the risk involved. Because such direct request data are not anonymous, the subject may wonder how direct he or she can be without creating ill will. It is generally less threatening to give feedback through suggestions rather than by declaring negative feelings.

## Subgroup Meetings

More anonymity results from dividing the staff into subgroups of three or four people that meet for thirty to forty-five minutes following a request like this: "I am very much concerned about my effectiveness as a manager. I would appreciate it if you all could help me at the next staff meeting by forming subgroups to identify my behaviors or any procedures that seem to reduce the effectiveness of our operation. I'd also like a list of things that you approve of and want me to continue. It would be helpful if you could give me concrete suggestions for improvement (identify the specific areas to be considered). I won't be present while you meet. You can turn in a written summary to my secretary. No names need be attached—I'm more interested in the information than in knowing its source. If any subgroup would like to talk with me directly, I'd welcome that opportunity."

## Total Group Meetings

It is possible for a manager to meet with the entire staff to discuss his or her managerial style and actions and to solicit suggestions for improvement. In such discussions, which usually are preplanned, the dialogue is more open than in the subgroup format; there can be more direct exchange between the manager and subordinates in an atmosphere of concern and mutual assistance. It is useful if the manager begins by sharing his or her own impressions of problem areas and asks for the subordinates' opinions.

The format can vary. The manager can summarize his or her impressions of his or her own style and ask for reactions from each person. The staff can form temporary subgroups and then resume a general discussion. When the manager and/or subordinates feel uneasy about sharing sensitive information, it is advisable to bring in a facilitator (change agent) to help direct the activities and prevent the group from moving into unproductive or difficult areas.

## Questionnaires

Written instruments provide another avenue for anonymous feedback. Here, the manager or personnel department circulates a questionnaire to gather data about the manager's performance as experienced by peers or subordinates. Available instruments include the Blake–Mouton Grid, Likert's Four Systems, Hall's Telometrics Instruments, and the Behavior Science Resources Management Profile.

Instrumented data can identify how the manager is perceived and how he or she could improve. Some instruments contain open-ended questions

("What does this person need to do to improve in this area?") that provide specific change alternatives.

The advantages of the instrumented process are that it can be widely administered, it focuses on common problems, it can be repeated at a later date, and it protects the anonymity of the respondents. Sometimes it's appropriate to hire an external change team to gather the data and then share it with those in the system for use in planning the change program.

## Shared Assessment

With this technique, the manager writes an assessment of his or her own performance and asks others to confirm or deny it, to share additional reactions, and to make suggestions for improvement. The following sample memo might be used.

**SAMPLE MEMO:** I have written the following assessment of my performance as a manager. Would you please indicate whether you agree or disagree with the various points, what your own reactions are, and what suggestions you have for improvement.
I feel I do the following things well:

1. I am punctual and never miss appointments or keep people waiting.
2. I am dependable in fulfilling assignments or requests.
3. I am a hard-working person with great loyalty to the company and its goals.

I also see the following negative things about my performance:

1. I am a rather closed person, and I don't communicate very much or very easily. I would like to improve this, but I'm not sure exactly how to do it.
2. I tend to cut people off in staff meetings and am somewhat rejecting of new ideas. I'm not exactly sure how people see or react to this.
3. People are a little afraid of me and feel a bit uncomfortable talking with me. (I don't know what gives people that impression or what I can do to reduce it.)

Space should be left under each of the comments for the reviewer's reactions and suggestions.

A form of shared assessment is used in performance review when the employee assesses his or her own performance and the superior reviews it. This becomes the basis for planning improved performance (Myers, 1972).

## Outside Consultant

An external consultant commonly is used for gathering feedback data. This person can come from outside the organization or from the company's training or personnel department, but rarely from the manager's department.

The consultant can use a variety of methods to gather feedback. He or she can observe the manager in action at meetings, in problem-solving sessions, or in the work setting. The consultant can also interview peers and subordinates or administer instruments and tabulate a summary profile.

The advantage of an outsider is that he or she often can see things to which insiders have become oblivious and can probe in areas not accessible to the manager. A disadvantage is that the manager and subordinates may become dependent on the consultant and never learn to give and receive helpful feedback as part of their ongoing relationship.

# After Feedback

For most people, sharing data with a superior is an especially high-risk activity. When it is first attempted, the employee usually watches closely to gauge the superior's reaction. And this reaction usually determines whether such feedback will be given again.

## Listen, Don't Explain or Justify

There is a tendency to explain or justify actions when we receive feedback that seems unwarranted or stems from a misunderstanding. When you ask for feedback, the burden is on you to listen and comprehend. This does not mean you are obligated to believe or accept the information; your responsibility is to try to understand why the other person feels and reacts that way. Defensive behavior usually stifles the flow of communication because it tells people you are more interested in justifying yourself than in understanding them.

## Ask for More

Especially in the open verbal feedback process, additional information might be forthcoming if the person eliciting the data can honestly keep saying, "That's extremely helpful. Tell me more. Is there anything else I should know about that?" This will support and encourage the continual flow of feedback.

## Check Out the Data

To make sure you have understood what the other person meant, it is helpful to summarize what you heard and ask if you understood correctly.

## Express Appreciation and Plan for the Future

Following feedback, you should acknowledge the risk that was involved for the person giving it and share your appreciation of his or her efforts. It also is a good time to plan future feedback sessions, which will probably be less disturbing and more productive than the initial encounter.

## Implications for Managing Change

Sometimes a negative impact in one's relationships with others results from an inability to translate one's intentions into appropriate behavior. At other times misperceptions lead to undesired consequences. In either case, the person initiating the interaction needs to discern the impact and explore his or her intentions and behavior filter, with the goal of reducing negative effects.

Gathering feedback is required for the improvement of impact. Several methods may be appropriate for stimulating a greater sharing of feedback from peers and subordinates. Personnel discussion, subgroups, written communication, instruments, and outside consultation assistance are available to the manager who is willing to initiate this sensitive, difficult, but much-needed process.

In the past, a great deal of attention has been devoted to the matter of how to *give* feedback. In the process of change, giving feedback is not as critical to the person who wants to improve his or her performance as the ability to gather feedback. It is virtually impossible to improve your performance if you don't know what you are doing that is ineffective. Therefore, the collecting of feedback is the beginning of change. It is important that the change agent or team examine current feedback mechanisms in the client organization. If these seem to be inadequate, a change program should begin with some feedback-gathering process for either an individual manager or an entire unit.

# CHAPTER 8
# Issues in Using Feedback as a Change Strategy

As people live and work together, they inevitably will be disturbed by one another's overt or covert behavior. Because we all have different physical makeups, personalities, temperaments, histories, attitudes, goals, habits, values, beliefs, motives, and needs, it would be virtually impossible to find any group whose behaviors were so perfectly matched as to preclude negative reactions.

On the assumption that people occasionally will find themselves at odds with someone else, how can one deal with these times of conflict? It seems natural to attempt to stop the person who is bothersome, whereupon he or she becomes a target of change. Feedback—informing the person that his or her behavior bothers us—is often initially employed in the hope that it will be sufficient impetus to provoke change.

Feedback may proceed something like this:

> **Sam:** Joe, you haven't said anything much at all in the last two meetings. I get quite anxious when you don't say anything. Why don't you speak up more? I really listen whenever you do say something.

> **Joe:** I speak up whenever I feel I have anything to contribute. I'm really a quiet person, and I just don't talk very much in groups this size.

Sam is giving appropriate feedback by telling Joe the effect of his behavior on others in a descriptive, nonjudgmental way. Basically, he is requesting that Joe change. When Joe learns that his silence makes others anxious, he feels a certain pressure to change his performance and to increase the quantity of his verbal contributions. Joe, however, could legitimately respond to the feedback this way:

> **Joe:** If my quietness bothers you, why don't you change? Why can't you learn to accept quiet people like me? Why do I have to change to make you feel better?

This presents a dilemma. Instead of expecting that Joe change as a result of feedback, Sam could alternatively assume that it is his own problem and try to accept Joe's behavior without giving feedback.

This dichotomy raises a number of questions: Are some behaviors so deep-rooted a part of one's personality that change is almost impossible? In that case, what are these behaviors? What behaviors are amenable to change? Should those who encounter unchangeable behaviors concentrate on widening their margin of acceptance rather than expecting change?

Following are a number of situations in which an individual's behavior was upsetting to other group members.

> June said she was "just naturally" a quiet person and did not speak up much in a group setting. Other group members did not accept this, so she was constantly encouraged to try to change her behavior. It seemed that some group members took it as a challenge to get June to become more vocal.
>
> Alice was told that people experienced her as a rather cold and distant person. Group members felt they could not relate easily to her and were not drawn to her. She was compared with Mary, who was seen as a warm, friendly person whom people liked and enjoyed. There was the direct implication that if Alice could be more like Mary, she would be a more effective person.
>
> Tom was blasted in the first round of feedback for his constant attempts to organize the group. He had pushed hard to get the group to identify its goals, to set up an agenda of activities, and to start working and not just sit around discussing whatever happened to come up. Tom said he worked better when things were organized, but the group said he pushed too hard, and they resented his attempts to structure them.
>
> Kathy was told that she seemed to avoid any conflict in the group. She was seen as always trying to smooth over difficulties, to agree with people quickly, and to avoid any confrontation with anyone. Kathy claimed that she liked to get along with people. She said she did not like arguments and discord and would rather go along with something with which she did not agree than provoke conflict.

Which of the above types represent behaviors that can or should be changed? In certain cases, the person exhibiting the problem behavior should be given feedback to initiate change. In other cases, the ones bothered by the behavior should devise an acceptance strategy.

If we give a person feedback about his or her behavior, what are the consequences? If Sam gives Joe feedback about his silence, what stance does Sam adopt while waiting for Joe to decide whether he wants to or can change? Does Sam just accept Joe the way he is whether he changes or not? In the latter case, why would Sam give Joe feedback at all—why not just accept Joe the way he already is?

And what about Joe? Having received feedback about his behavior, what should he do? He knows that Sam is bothered; if he doesn't change, how will Sam feel about him? Is Sam sitting back waiting for some sign of change?

If you ask people if they want to be accepted the way they are, they usually say something like this: "Yes, I wish people could accept *me* as the person I am. I don't like to feel that people accept me only if I conform to the image of what they want. If I feel accepted, I am inclined to listen if they point out something in my behavior I should change to be more effective."

*Acceptance* implies accepting a person the way he or she is, not the way we would like him or her to be. It could be argued that if such acceptance is essential for building trust, the basic process in human interaction is the constant expansion of one's own margin of acceptance of others. Feedback, in the sense of provoking change, would be superfluous. If feedback directed toward change is a basic interaction process, what is it about another person we accept? If we accept this behavior and not that one, what determines the value of each?

Here we face an important issue of values. What we do or do not accept in the behavior of others depends, in part, on what we value and what we consider right. If a person engages in behaviors that we find unacceptable, it would seem that we should examine our value system to see whether we can alter the values upon which our reaction is based. If that is not possible, we may need to engage in a feedback process that potentially leads to behavior change. Some values may not be central to a person's identity or sense of personal integrity, while other values may be basic to a person's sense of self and therefore be difficult to change.

What kinds of behaviors in the examples given above would represent unacceptable behaviors—behaviors that would violate a *basic* value? The two situations with value implications involve Tom and Kathy. Tom's desire to control people and impose his ideas and opinions on others violates some people's values. Although Tom might see himself as just "well organized," those who experience him as manipulative should engage in direct feedback pertaining to the issue between them.

Kathy considers herself a pleasant person who likes to get along with people. To her co-workers, however, she is someone who pretends not to have any particular feelings but in fact leans strongly in certain directions. This would lead to feedback from those whose values she violates through her hypocrisy, as they see it.

After carefully determining that increased acceptance is an inadequate solution, the person whose values are violated should initiate feedback. At times, it may be appropriate to respond to a request for feedback and share negative feelings even though no values have been violated, because the person initiating the request has a right to find out how his or her behavior affects others. The feedback data should specify whether the behavior just "bothers" one or whether it is experienced as a violation of certain basic values.

Feedback, then, is not merely a request for change in behavior, but the beginning of a process of acceptance or change. It is not uncommon for a group that has given feedback to observe a significant change in a short time—change that an outside observer probably would not have detected. Interestingly enough, following a feedback session, previous "bothersome" behavior is no longer such a source of irritation. This suggests that one of the critical functions of feedback is the initiation of acceptance; it seems that we can accept behavior much more readily if we can talk about it openly and if the person receiving the feedback is willing to hear it and take it into account. In this sense, feedback leads to wider acceptance of others.

However, recent research (Tavris, 1982) indicates some important implications of feedback that's prompted by anger. Carol Tavris writes in *Psychology Today*, "A sociologist in the field of family violence finds that couples who yell at each other do not thereafter feel less angry but more angry. Verbal aggression and physical aggression were highly correlated . . . which means that it is a small step from bitter accusations to slaps. Leonard Berkowitz, who has studied the social causes of aggression for many years, likewise finds that ventilation by yelling has no effect on [reducing] anger. 'Telling someone we hate him will supposedly purge pent-up aggressive inclinations and will clear the air,' he says. Frequently, however, when we tell someone off, we stimulate ourselves to continued or even stronger aggression." (p. 32)

Giving feedback in anger may result in increased unhappiness and a wider rift in the relationship. The goal of feedback should be to increase acceptance between people, not just giving vent to pent-up anger.

One widely discussed issue in the arena of acceptance addresses whether it is possible to accept a person without necessarily accepting that person's behaviors. In the above analysis, it is suggested that before one rejects or refuses to accept another's behavior, one should examine the criteria for nonacceptance; if the behavior represents the violation of an important value, one has more reason to initiate action directed toward changing the other person. But if one rejects the behavior of another because of personal preferences or idiosyncratic factors, then perhaps one should try to change one's own preferences and try to accept the behavior without trying to change the other person. It is vital to adopt an appropriate change strategy only after having assessed the cause of the problems between people.

If the behavior under consideration does violate a central value and is therefore unacceptable, does rejection of the behavior constitute a rejection of the person? Is it possible to accept the liar and reject the lying? This is a very difficult question in that rejecting behaviors central to the identity of a person may be tantamount to rejecting the person. Hearing "I accept you but I cannot accept your ultraconservative attitudes" may indicate general rejection to someone whose conservatism is critical to his or her identity. If one rejects one part of another's behavior, it would seem almost mandatory to increase accepting and supportive behavior in other areas. This leads to a practical principle: If one gives feedback to a person indicating nonacceptance of a behavior, one must increase one's accepting behavior towards that person in general.

## Implications of Managing Change

Although all change strategies are concerned with getting someone to change his or her behavior, personal and interpersonal issues are often the most sensitive. It is one thing to try to improve someone's attendance at meetings; it is quite another matter to persuade that person to be less "bossy" or dogmatic. Those trying to achieve change in others' personal behaviors often use a feedback process. Too often, feedback comes across as a demand for change rather than a request to explore the relationship. The person giving feedback should be willing to consider the alternatives of altering his or her values or expanding his or her acceptance instead of just expecting the other person to change. Giving feedback can be an act of tyranny or selfishness. It can actually mean, "I give you feedback and I want you to change because I have power in our relationship, and I will feel better if you change."

Before a change agent initiates a feedback session in the client system, the function of feedback should be discussed in depth. It should be emphasized that feedback begins an exploration of relationships—it is not just a demand that others change.

# CHAPTER 9
# Congruent High-Trust Behavior: A Change Goal and Process

Probably nothing damages a manager's effectiveness more than mistrust. When subordinates do not trust their bosses, they tend to withhold data, become suspicious of decisions and programs, and expend their energies protecting themselves rather than engaging in creative or productive work. Therefore, a low level of trust between people is often an immediate target for change.

One reason people are not trusted is that their behavior is incongruent: they *say* one thing, but their nonverbal behavior (facial responses, body language) conveys a different message. For example, a manager may say he trusts a subordinate, yet he checks up on every assignment, demands inconsequential details, and hovers over the employee's desk. There is an obvious incongruity between what the manager says and what he does. To improve the level of trust, it is important to understand the basis of congruent behavior and how to move from incongruent actions to congruency.

## Congruent Behavior

The idea of congruence as described by Carl Rogers (1961) has generated excited acceptance as well as disturbing criticism in the management field. Rogers defines congruence as "the term we have used to indicate an accurate matching of experiencing and awareness. It may still be further extended to cover a matching of experience, awareness, and communication. Perhaps the simplest example is an infant. If he is experiencing hunger at the physiological and visceral level, then his awareness appears to match his experience, and his communication is also congruent with his experience" (p. 308).

Rogers goes on to point out the disruption that occurs in a relationship in which there is noncongruent behavior. If a person whom I think is angry denies her anger, I become wary and distrustful of her. On the other hand, if she admits the anger that is consistent with my experience of her, then I feel she is an honest, trustworthy person; my confidence increases and the relationship develops around feelings of trust and openness. Thus, according to Rogers (1961), congruence leads to the following general principle:

> The greater the congruence of experience, awareness, and communication on the part of one individual, the more the ensuing relationship will involve: a tendency toward more mutually accurate understanding of the communication; improved psychological adjustment and functioning in both parties; mutual satisfaction in the relationship. . . .

> Conversely, the greater the communicated incongruence of experience and awareness, the more the ensuing relationship will involve: further communication with the same quality; disintegration of accurate understanding; less adequate psychological adjustment and functioning in both parties; and mutual dissatisfaction in the relationship (p. 313).

In presenting this idea to individuals and groups—while indicating my own acceptance of the general concept of congruent behavior—I usually confront three main objections:

1. "Do you mean that people should always behave exactly as they feel? If I feel like punching you in the nose, abusing your wife, or yelling obscenities at you, should I go ahead?" The issue raised here is this: *Does congruence mean giving in to all impulses immediately?*
2. "I have been taught all my life that I should learn to control my anger or negative feelings. Suppose I don't like someone; if I behave as though I do like him or her, then I think I will begin to like him or her. Suppose I feel unhappy; if I try to act happy, after a while I will feel happier." The issue here is this: *If I behave congruently all the time, will I ever learn to improve on those behaviors in myself that I do not like?*
3. Congruence sounds good, but it doesn't work. I told my wife the other night that I was really upset with how sloppy I find the house when I come home from work. She was so mad she didn't speak to me for three days, and I had to plead for forgiveness and buy her a present and behave in all kinds of noncongruent ways before we got back on an even keel." The issue here is this: *Congruence does not always seem to result in immediate improvement in relationships. Why not?*

## Issue One: Does Congruence Mean License?

Does congruence mean that it is all right for a person to behave in any way that is consistent with his or her current state of awareness and experience? Congruence in this direct and immediate sense *has* become a major value for those who stress the hypocrisy of "society" and the lack of congruence they observe in conventional life. They feel people would be more effective in the long run if they were aware of their feelings and expressed them openly and immediately rather than hiding or denying them.

Psychiatrist Eric Berne (1964) popularized the superficial game-playing that characterizes many human interactions. The "games people play" are the opposite of congruent behavior, and it is such phony behavior that has prompted the notion of congruence as an antidote to hypocrisy.

We seem to be living in an emotionally deprived culture in which the emphasis is on rational behavior to the detriment of emotional response. Two writers on organizational behavior, Argyris (1962) and Gibb (1965), have pointed out that the dominance of rationality in the management of many organizations has disruptive consequences insofar as unacknowledged emotional behavior interferes with ongoing activities. Many observers of this denial of emotional behavior in organizations suggest that managers need to learn to recognize, accept, and deal more effectively with human emotions. In this sense they are prescribing congruence—more open emotion and a greater willingness to deal with emotion openly and honestly—rather than the prevailing norms that support phoniness, maintenance of a facade, gamesmanship, and denial of feelings.

Congruence is based on value orientations already present in traditional society. For example, in *King Lear*, Shakespeare says, "Speak what we feel, not what we ought to say." As mentioned above, going overboard with congruency is less of a problem for most people than overcontrolled nonemotional behavior.

Equating congruence with license stems from the assumption that congruence becomes the only value a person lives by, or at least the major value. But values are interdependent. Congruency has been suggested as a new value without examining in any depth the other values people hold. When we look at our value systems, we may find there are some values we should relinquish as no longer useful and others we should cherish and retain.

When I am asked whether I advocate behaving exactly as one feels even if one feels like hitting someone, I answer in this manner: "Being congruent is not the only value I hold. I also value the rights of others. My personal value system calls for a society based on mutual respect and acceptance. If I were to engage in behavior that might be 'congruent' at the moment, I would violate a great many other values that I deem important. I will not violate those values just to be congruent."

The issue then becomes how to deal with hostile, punishing, or devastating feelings. If I were to act them out directly, I would violate other important values. If I repress feelings, I may suffer from psychosomatic problems or manifest subtle, hostile reactions toward others. Thus, my definition of congruence would encourage me to express my feelings without necessarily acting them out. However, this behavior leads to the problem raised in issue two.

## Issue Two: Does Congruence Allow for Change?

Congruence in its simplest form requires that each person behave according to his or her current level of awareness and experience. Sometimes we are not happy with that level; we would prefer not to feel the way we sometimes do. We would like to change.

From time to time I encounter a person who considers his or her personality to be fixed and almost unchangeable. Therefore, he or she should not be held responsible, because "this is the way I am." This attitude reminds me of the story of the scorpion who asked a frog to carry him across a stream:

"No," said the frog, "you'll sting me if I do."

"Of course not," replied the scorpion. "If I do, you will sink and we will both be lost."

At that, the frog agreed to ferry the scorpion across the water. In the middle of the stream, the scorpion suddenly jabbed the frog with a fatal sting. With his last breath, the frog asked, "Why did you do it?"

Replied the scorpion, "It's in my nature."

People are not scorpions (although some act the part), and we have learned that human nature is not fixed or unchangeable. Anyone who says, "I'm just a blunt person; if that hurts you, it's just the way I am," apparently operates on the scorpion theory of personality. The congruence theory would seem to give this type of person the perfect rationale to continue behaviors that reflect "just the way I am" regardless of their consequences for others.

For those who hold a complex of values, an experience often elicits a range of feelings at variance with each other. To which feeling should one be congruent? Suppose I feel so hostile toward another person that I feel like punching him in the nose. At the same time, another set of values elicits guilt about the hostility, reminds me that I should try to love my neighbor as myself, and urges me to understand and accept others as they are. Despite my hostile feelings, I do not want to live my life responding in impulsive, hostile, punishing ways toward others. I do not want to adopt the scorpion justification that "this is just the way I am." Certain values suggest change. Although congruency *seems* to have a nonchange orientation, congruency in a more complete sense, in my experience, becomes the real basis for change.

After all, if I feel hostile toward another person and simultaneously experience concern or guilt for feeling that way in light of other values, congruency theory would require that I share *all* these feelings, not just the hostile ones. If I were truly congruent (which demands that I be aware of *all* my own values and emotions), I would express myself something like this: "John, when you try to dominate the meeting, I want to punch you in the nose. You make me feel very hostile and angry. But I don't like to feel that way. I would like to accept you and work with you. How can I work out these feelings with you?"

Accepting and admitting that we have negative feelings does not mean that we want to keep them or that we cannot change. My own experience tells me that expressing the feelings that I do not like and want to change— revealing them to the person in question—decreases these feelings and allows me to experience my positive feelings. Should I go so far as to act as though I like someone I dislike, in the hope that this will make me like him? In light of the discussion above, the answer is no. I should share with him both my feelings of dislike and my desire to like him and engage in a continual interaction to allow the positive feelings to be enhanced. That would be the result if there is any validity to the Homans proposition from the group dynamics field that liking increases with interaction (Homans, 1961).

There is also the matter of timing. Does congruency demand that I express all my feelings immediately? Many people find that if they "sleep on it" they feel different. Some theories of personality suggest that the passage of time does not eliminate feelings but, rather, allows them to become buried in the unconscious. Others maintain that through insight and self-dialogue we can resolve our feelings without expressing them to others.

Can one be congruent if one admits one's feelings to oneself but does not share them immediately and openly with the others involved? Can one wrestle with one's own feelings and the relevant sets of values and win a private war, or does congruency demand an open interaction? I think I have experienced both conditions. I think I have been able to examine silently my own conflicting feelings and achieve a sense of resolution or congruence, if you will, within myself. On the other hand, I have also participated (usually in a training setting) in the exciting process of immediately revealing to another person my feelings about his or her behavior and then working through our differences. In my experience, this has led to the deepening of the relationship that Rogers described. It may be that the private, one-sided resolution of feelings toward another does not enhance the relationship but does result in a personal sense of satisfaction.

One theory of emotional behavior contends that unexpressed emotions persist and intensify if the reason for them continues. For example, one may be irritated by another until he finally "can't stand it any longer," whereupon there is an explosion of feeling that actually may be stronger than was originally warranted. Thus, it would seem that resolution of certain interpersonal conflicts would result more easily if the problems are dealt with immediately. It would also seem that if we were more congruent in the earlier stage of the emotional experience, initial feelings would more accurately represent our reaction to the stimulus behavior. Then again, waiting may allow us to cool down and more adequately express a range of feelings and values. As mentioned earlier, recent research indicates that anger, if immediately expressed, reinforces the angry feelings rather than dissipating them. The best strategy for managing anger seems to be an examination of the reasons for the anger and the formulation of a problem-solving response.

Managers who desire to become more congruent should look at their current style of managing people. A manager who continually represses his or her feelings about the performance of subordinates may need to be more open. On the other hand, if a manager reacts too quickly to others and creates a climate of conflict, more internal dialogue before response may be more appropriate.

## Issue Three: Can Congruence Be Learned?

People have differing ways or differing styles of behaving congruently. Congruent behavior for Person A may be perceived as crude, blunt, and punishing, whereas Person B's behavior, also congruently oriented, may appear open, helpful, and trustworthy. Is there some element of skill in behavior? Is it possible to communicate better and elicit reactions from others more in line with our intentions toward them? The purpose of a training program is not only to help participants examine a new value such as congruency and see how it fits into their value structure but also to help them develop skill in implementing this new value.

Argyris (1962) points out an important factor in giving helpful feedback: namely, that feedback remain descriptive and nonevaluative. The same qualities apply to all attempts at congruent behavior—that is, we must learn to express our feelings in descriptive, nonevaluative terms. One might say, "When you did this [describe the action], it made me feel this way [describe as accurately as possible the inner state you experience]."

People worried about congruent behavior ask, "How can I present my feelings tactfully so I don't hurt anyone?" or "If I think through what I am going to say and choose my words carefully, will I avoid problems?" Careful planning often results in speeches that sound guarded, cautious, rehearsed, and anything but authentic, congruent communication. The descriptive formula allows for more immediate, spontaneous congruency.

It should also be recognized that human interaction takes place in a social structure in which social norms and expectations may inhibit a positive response even if we are skillfully congruent. Within the context of the social system, each person has a defined position or status and a role definition. Some people in subordinate roles have reported returning from a human relations laboratory and trying new congruent behaviors with disconcerting results: The superiors continue to expect the old sub-servient behavior. New congruent behaviors, if unexpected, are perceived as threatening, and evoke a negative response. When there is little system support for the new congruent behaviors, one reluctantly abandons the new congruency for the old, more rewarded role behaviors.

Here, then, is a real dilemma for someone suddenly confronted with the new value of congruency. It may be very appealing, and he or she may want to adopt it. However, those at home, work, church, or the community setting are not oriented toward this new value and expect him or her to perform as he or she has done in the past. Rewards will be contingent on a continuation of expected behaviors.

Thus, the young husband who suddenly begins to behave congruently may be seriously violating a set of interaction expectations developed with his wife over a long period of time. It would be surprising if she responded positively from the first. The couple needs to develop a whole new set of norms, roles, and expectations. The congruency theory assumes that the best way to manage this change is for the husband to begin the new behaviors and then work through the consequences with his wife. Other models suggest that the change agent (the husband, in this case) should not impose change, but that change procedures should be a collaborative effort agreed upon by both. It is not uncommon for a husband or wife who has attended a training laboratory to ask the spouse to attend so that together they can begin a new pattern of behavior based on a common frame of reference. Many organizations send teams of managers to training programs so that they can adopt new behaviors based on a common new experience. Even if they have not all attended a common training program, a team can begin to explore new ways of behavior and establish congruent new norms if the manager is willing to support new behaviors.

## Implications for Managing Change

In this discussion I have been addressing some of the problems a person who adopts a new value of congruency may expect to encounter. If these conditions are recognized, congruent behavior may be successful. The assumption is that low congruency creates mistrust; if one wishes to change the trust level, the congruency condition is an important focus of change.

1. Congruency is not the only value a person holds. To be congruent, one must behave consistently with old values or begin to reevaluate one's value system and abandon or modify old values.
2. If one's values are in contradiction, the congruency stance is an effective method of changing them. That is, one can verbalize the ambivalence one feels about holding contradictory values and involve others in the process of examining the problems that result.
3. Congruency does not mean that people cannot change. Certain values may support behaviors that we like better than others, even if we do not feel or behave in the desired way now. By expressing our current feelings and also our desire for improvement, we initiate a process that helps us move toward the desired behavior goals.

4. Congruent behavior may take more skill than one now possesses. Learning to be congruent via a descriptive rather than an evaluative process may result in more positive response from others.
5. The social systems within which interaction takes place may be resistant to new congruent behaviors. Structured role definitions and expectations may need to be altered before reciprocal congruency can be engaged in at all.
6. If incongruency is causing a low trust level in a client system, the change agent should model highly congruent behavior if there is any expectation that the client system will change.

# CHAPTER 10
# Achieving Interdependence

Somewhere between the chaos of anarchy and the tyranny that insists on total obedience lies the realm of interdependence. In the field of organizations and management it represents the balance between those in authority and their subordinates. Interdependence is also present between peers when each can rely on the resources of the other. Interdependent people acknowledge both their own strengths and shortcomings and those of others, and are willing to cooperate to achieve common goals. Such cooperation is to be desired, for it allows everyone to participate, to feel important because he or she is important, and to accomplish the purposes of the organization. Often, a change agent attempts to help others break out of crippling dependency or destructive counterdependency and to create an interdependent balance.

Consider the following example of a new employee:

> Tom is new on the job. He feels he is intelligent and capable and that with time and experience he will be a good salesman. But at the same time he is scared—he doesn't want to make mistakes. Running through his mind are two contradictory questions about his course of action: "Shall I tell the sales manager that I feel I need someone to help me? Or shall I just strike out on my own and prove to everyone that I can do as good a job as anyone else? Will others interpret my asking for help as a sign of weakness? If I do ask for help, will they let me handle things my own way later on?" Tom sits, pondering, deep in his dilemma.

## Conflicting Needs

Two crosscurrents are present in all of us—the need to be free, independent, and capable of doing things on our own, and the need to be dependent, to have the luxury of putting ourselves into the hands of others when our own resources are insufficient.

Depending on his or her degree of self-knowledge and understanding of the staff, a manager who observes these apparently conflicting needs in others will respond in ways that may or may not result in the growth of a particular subordinate. It is *from* the authority figure that the subordinate is trying to break free to demonstrate his or her own competence, and it is *to* the authority figure he or she must go for support and assistance. Central to the performance of any leader—supervisor or executive—is the manner and method employed to respond to the needs of others.

## Dependence

Some managers' styles of behavior reinforce and support the dependency of their subordinates, with the long-range consequence that the subordinates remain incapable of functioning adequately on their own. For example, Sam Wilson drops into his boss's office almost every day to "talk things over" and solicit an opinion on his work. These regular visits, which have taken place for some years, are very satisfying to Sam. He feels his boss likes to be consulted and asked for advice, and he believes that the daily consultation has kept him from making some pretty serious mistakes.

Sam's example contains several elements of a strong dependency-development relationship. The person in the authority position (in this case the boss) may be using the subordinate to meet many of his own needs. The boss probably would be indignant and hurt if it were suggested that he was selfish; selfishness (in the sense of concern about himself at someone else's expense) is not part of his conscious motivation. But in a real sense this boss has unknowingly been meeting his own needs without considering the long-range well-being of Sam.

There are times when dependency is legitimate and useful. Occasions will arise in which a person needs help beyond his or her own resources. All of us must depend on others—doctors, teachers, counselors, friends, parents—when we confront conditions that are beyond our ability to handle effectively alone. Dependency becomes crippling when a person no longer seeks to develop his or her own resources and to move to a more collaborative stance with those in authority but automatically assumes he or she can do nothing without the guidance, support, and influence of others.

All human beings start life in a position of almost complete dependency on others. The development of the child's self-sufficiency is the responsibility of the adults who occupy positions of authority over him or her. *How to use authority to help others grow is a major challenge for every person in a position of authority.*

Too often those in authority have the wrong goals—parents want children who are well behaved; teachers want quiet classrooms filled with students who will do and say what they're told; administrators want subordinates who will obey without question, who are "good soldiers." One way to achieve these goals is to create dependency in others. Interestingly enough, many dependency-producing leaders never recognize their part in the problem, for they often say sadly, "What we need is more people who take initiative and won't just sit around waiting to be told what to do."

## Counterdependence

Another part of this behavioral stream is the desire to be free, to "do it by myself." Some, such as the English philosopher Thomas Hobbes, have postulated that by his very nature each person is at war with everyone else as each tries to hammer out his or her own ego-centered world. If everyone actually were to do only what he or she wanted, without taking others into account, the result would be anarchy.

Supervisors who see in their subordinates the tendency to seek freedom may try to stifle, reduce, or change that tendency. There may be subtle (and sometimes not so subtle) struggle between the leaders, who want to channel or control, and the subordinates, who want to be more independent and do the job as they feel it should be done. It is this basic struggle that underlies counterdependency. Some people expend much time and energy finding ways to resist authority; they can justify to themselves why the desires of the authority figure can't or shouldn't be carried out, and they act accordingly.

Sometimes a negative response results from the wrong approach by the authority figure. Perhaps he or she initiates directions in a demeaning way that robs the subordinate of personal dignity. Often no allowance is made for questions, discussion, or dialogue; the boss wants the worker to obey "with no back talk." Such an attitude may create a strong resistant reaction. In the same vein, a dominating leader may deliberately create situations where the subordinate questions or resists so that he or she can "show who is boss."

It should not be assumed, however, that resistance and reaction are always the fault of the authority figure. Even when the superior is behaving appropriately, the subordinate, conditioned to resent and rebel against authority, nevertheless responds negatively. Sometimes, in order to achieve a new and more effective level of interaction, both subordinate and authority figure must reexamine their attitudes and behavior and work out a change.

## How to Develop Interdependence

An ideal relationship that is both possible and desirable between authority and subordinates is called *interdependence*—the cooperative or collaborative use of each other's resources. Independence is not the appropriate term, for it suggests that the subordinate is freed from those in authority and goes his or her own way. Independence is not the most effective condition for existing in today's world—whether it be in family, school, church, business or government organization, community, or nation. Of necessity we are an interdependent people. Unfortunately, many people have not learned to be interdependent successfully.

## Implications for Managing Change

Following are some important actions to be taken by people in authority who wish to encourage greater interdependence. A change agent may find the problem of dependency relevant in two areas. When the change agent is trying to alter his or her own tendencies to dominate and foster dependence in the client, the issue is to help the client become more interdependent with the change agent or change team. When the change agent working in an organization observes crippling dependency or counterdependency, he or she should help people break out of their unhealthy patterns.

## Care and Concern

One important condition connected with improving interdependent behavior is the personal concern exhibited by the person in authority towards the subordinate. A subordinate must know that the authority figure really cares about him or her, not just about whether he or she follows orders. Much organizational research has emphasized high concern for people as a critical factor in successful management (Likert, 1961).

Concern for the individual should be unconditional, although we may not care for certain of his or her actions. Too many authority figures present conditional concern as the basis of a relationship: "I will accept you only on condition that you do what I want, remain dependent on me, and meet my needs." Such a basis probably results in either dependency or rebellion. As part of a change plan, the change agent may need to explore the level of concern in the organization—how much real concern is apparent and how is it handled?

## Trust

Authority figures should have greater confidence and trust in those under them. Leaders should trust their subordinates to make correct decisions and should give them the opportunity to do so. The authority who is fearful that others will make mistakes or won't do the job his or her way hovers around, watching and checking up, and makes everyone self-conscious and resentful. Delegation depends on trust; subordinates' growth cannot flourish if they are never trusted to try something new or to assume greater responsibility.

Trust means allowing—allowing others to perform with a sense of confidence that they are supported by the person over them. Trust means being consistent and trustworthy so that those being directed have confidence in the words and actions of the authority figure. The building of trust may become part of the change goal as one tries to increase the level of interdependency.

## Open Communication

A vital ingredient in interdependence is the open sharing of information. Communication implies an understanding between sender and recipient that operates in both directions. Interdependence is not a one-way communication system in which the authority tells and others are always supposed to listen. On almost every subject, people have thoughts, ideas, or opinions as well as feelings. If we want true understanding, we must share both kinds of data.

Many leaders share few of their feelings or ideas with others. Giving directions, orders, and commands is *not* sharing. Sharing comes first, before decisions are made; when the authority figure says, "I want to know what you think and how you feel about the issue at hand. I will not judge you or punish you for being truthful and candid. If we can all put our cards on the table, and if we really have concern and trust for one another, we can come up with solutions that will be satisfying to all."

## Shared Decisions

Interdependence requires that decisions be made in a collaborative way, with all participants understanding one another and coming to a solution they approve and are willing to support. Shared decisions are not necessarily fifty-fifty decisions, in the sense that each person will demand an equal part. Sometimes the manager will say to a subordinate, "You have more experience with this problem than I do; I trust you to make the decision, and I'll support it." At other times the subordinate will respond similarly to the boss or each will listen to the other and work out a solution both can support and implement. Some decisions should be made by the authority figure alone, some following consultation with others, and some as a result of general participation.

In diagnosing the health of an organization, the change team will want to examine the decision-making procedures. If sharing is inadequate, training in decision-making methods would be an appropriate change action.

## Joint Action

Interdependence means working together, which is necessary to carry out decisions. In too many organizations, leaders *tell* their workers what to do and pressure, control, or punish until their demands are met. Subordinates are denied the delight of a team effort, the accomplishment of things done collaboratively. Sometimes work requires solitary effort, but it is more satisfying if it can be shared.

We see all around us the consequences of people in rebellion. Either they are in revolt against authority, or they have never learned to work with authority figures. Training in collaborative problem-solving and team effort should be taught in the home but can be learned on the job. Interdependence does not mean that leaders allow others license to do whatever they please, nor does it mean that subordinates slavishly carry out the whims of their leaders. Rather, it is a matter of mutual effort based on concern and trust. When these conditions do not exist, the building of interdependency becomes an important change goal.

# CHAPTER 11

# Reducing Role Conflicts and Stress

One of the critical issues in modern organizational life is personal anxiety and stress. Health problems, especially heart disease, as well as diminished work performance, have been found to be associated with conflicts people experience in balancing the multitude of roles they are expected to enact (French and Caplan, 1972).

For many change agents, helping others to reduce role conflicts and stress may be an important change goal. A number of organizations conduct programs in stress management as part of a change strategy to keep their key personnel functioning effectively.

Nearly all people observe that as they move from one situation or set of relationships to another, their behavior changes. One does not behave the same way in church as one does at work, at home, at a party, or at a lodge meeting. Each situation entails specific demands to which most people readily respond. In social science parlance, each different set of responses—the behavior that is expected in a given situation—is a role. Complexity and confusion ensue as people multiply the number of roles they must assume without recognizing the forces at work and the stress and strain that inevitably occur.

First, it is important to note that in each situation where one assumes a role, the others involved have at their disposal the power to reward or punish to the degree one fulfills or fails to fulfill one's role obligations. If a subordinate does not fulfill his or her work role properly (carrying out assignments, getting work done on time), the boss may apply punishment through a reprimand or denial of certain benefits or rewards.

Second, it should be recognized that most people internalize the demands of a role; that is, the expected role behavior becomes a part of the need system of the individual. In order to maintain one's self-respect, respect from others, and feeling of adequacy and self-worth, one must perform the roles that have been accepted. If a person who has internalized a role does not conform to its demands, he or she punishes him- or herself with feelings of guilt or self-effacement even though no one is present to apply external punishment. Thus, a young woman who drinks with the group to win its approval will suffer pangs of guilt because she has violated the demands of her role as a church member. A salesman who pads his expense account because others do it loses self-respect because his action violates his conception of honesty.

Punishment or reward, then, may stem from other persons or from within oneself. People are generally very sensitive to their own reactions and try consciously or unconsciously to maintain conditions in which there is a maximum of reward and a minimum of punishment. One must recognize, of course, that individuals differ in their definitions of reward and punishment.

Problems and conflict arise when a person is caught in a situation that involves reward and punishment. This is the basis of role conflict: the same behavior brings both positive and negative responses either within oneself or from others, thereby creating stress. Role conflict can be divided into two general classes: conflict of multiple roles and conflict inherent in one role. These, in turn, can be subdivided. Conflicts between roles can be a conflict of norms or a conflict of time. Conflict within a role can be conflict of time, of skill, or of expectations.

# Multiple-Role Conflict

## Disparity between Group Norms

A common source of serious conflict lies in the disparity between the demands of two concurrent roles one person is expected to take. A teenager often finds that his or her role within the peer group requires different behavior from that demanded by his or her role at home or as a church member. Stealing hubcaps may elicit the approval of the gang but brings swift disapproval from the parent or minister. Research evidence has documented the dilemma of the foreman who finds himself caught between the demands of his worker friends and his new role as a representative of management. If the foreman behaves in ways that satisfy the friends, he may be violating the requirements of his duties. The reverse is also possible.

Essentially, the conflict arises because of the group norms, from which roles are derived. The norms of group A may demand certain actions, and the norms of group B may press for diametrically opposed behavior. This situation involves conflicting pressures from others as well as personal conflict within the individual who is oriented to both sets of norms. He or she may feel guilty about behaving a certain way even if the other group is unaware of the "deviant" behavior.

This type of conflict is experienced by many people: a businessman engaged in cutthroat business practices plagued by Judeo-Christian ethics insisting that he love his neighbor as himself; a student pressured by classmates to cheat in spite of home and church norms; or a member of a Republican family who belongs to a Democratic social group.

How do people handle this type of role conflict? Obviously not everyone afflicted with multiple roles cracks up under the strain. A number of protective psychological devices are used. Some employ various defense mechanisms such as rationalization or repression—that is, they make acceptable excuses for their contrary behavior or try not to think about it. Others compartmentalize; they put each role in a separate mental compartment and refuse to acknowledge any conflict. A fortunate few are able to withdraw from one of their roles in light of a priority of values. Many, unable to eliminate any conflicting roles, continue to operate burdened by stress, anxiety, pressure, and guilt feelings.

## "Time Crunch"

Time conflict, another type of multiple-role conflict, is the common phenomenon of a person assuming so many roles in so many groups that he or she cannot possibly fulfill all the obligations involved. Someone in this situation may receive rewards from one group for spending time on their program while experiencing negative pressures from another group for not having spent time with them. The classic example is the man who succeeds professionally but is berated by his family for being away so much. It is common for people in organizations to accept all assignments offered and then wind up in time binds as each assignment demands more time and energy.

Aware of the universal pressure on the overloaded person, each group tries to apply the most pressure. Fortunate is he or she who can evaluate the many roles and eliminate or redefine some of them to reduce the conflict and tension level. Listing the roles, assessing their demands and time requirements, and deciding which ones are central to one's personal goals should help in reducing conflicts.

# Internal Role Conflict

## Time and Ability

When conflict occurs within a single role, the time factor again is involved. It is often closely tied to multiple group membership, for a person accepts a role for which he or she has time and that causes no conflict with any other role and then discovers that it demands actions that he or she does not have the ability to undertake. A person too shy and retiring to refuse a role as fund-raiser in a volunteer organization may be terrified at the prospect of visiting people to ask them for money. She may devise all kinds of reasons why she doesn't have time to carry out the assignment, or she may complete the task, detesting it all along and refusing to assist the organization again.

From this analysis, one would naturally assume that the wisest course would be to match role demands with skills and ability. This is easier said than done. On the one hand, it is possible that someone may have the latent ability and could grow with the job despite feelings of inadequacy. On the other hand, a person may be confident and willing but not incompetent in actual performance.

The acceptance of a role for which a person feels he or she does not have the necessary skills may result in rewards from the group, accompanied by pressure and self-doubt that are very real and very painful.

## Failure to Fulfill Others' Expectations

Finally, a person may experience conflict because different people have differing expectations as to how his or her role should be carried out. A teacher may find that some parents expect her to be a strict disciplinarian, and others feel she should be permissive and accepting. By performing her role one way, she receives the approval of one set of parents but angry reactions from the other. A reversal of behavior does not solve the problem. This type of conflict is even more frustrating when expectations are not defined, so that the person receives negative reactions without knowing what he or she has done to elicit them. A person new to the management position often experiences this kind of conflict when his or her boss expects one type of performance and his or her peer group applies subtle pressure for contrary actions. The spouse may have a widely differing conception of the manager's role, and former superiors may have taught yet another view. Finally, subordinates have their own views as to how the manager should function. Research on the role of the supervisor clearly shows that supervisors themselves, their bosses, and their subordinates all have differing expectations (Dyer, 1983).

As this old tale illustrates, it is obviously impossible to meet everyone's expectations when they are all different: A couple with a donkey found that someone was sure to complain if one or the other rode the donkey, if both rode, or if no one rode. In trying to satisfy everyone, the couple wound up carrying the donkey—a ridiculous adjustment to the situation. It is apparent that this type of conflict is difficult to resolve, especially when each faction feels its expectations are legitimate. Sometimes it is possible to change people's expectations. Sometimes one must perform the role as he or she thinks it should be done despite the demands of others, thereby decreasing inner conflicts without eliminating external pressures.

If we put together all the role-conflict situations mentioned above, it becomes apparent that this is indeed a very complex society. Imagine a person with too many roles, some of which represent opposing group norms, some of which demand actions for which he has inadequate skills, and some of which represent responses to conflicting expectations. In each case, others are applying constant pressure to get him to fulfill the role as they define it, and at the same time he himself is suffering from feelings of inadequacy and guilt.

## Implications for Managing Change

A person who experiences role conflict in any of its forms often needs assistance in sorting out his or her roles and making decisions as to priorities and actions. This assistance may become a major goal of the change agent or change team. It is impossible to work out conflicts until one has clearly described his or her goals. Following goal-setting, it is possible to establish priorities that will help in reducing time conflicts. If one also establishes a list of groups or systems according to priority, one can sort out problems of expectations. The next step is to devise a plan to eliminate low-priority activities even though they may involve people or activities one enjoys or to whom one feels obligation.

Values are also important. Role conflicts will continue until one has clearly determined his or her basic values. Conflict resolution goes deep, for a person must wrestle with such fundamental issues as: What are my goals? What are my values? What are my priorities? Afterward he or she may deal with taking risks, saying no, and taking positive action to bring order out of conflict.

At times, the change agent can help in the resolution of conflicts by bringing together parties who are putting pressure on others or who have contrary expectations of one person. If these parties are powerful or important, it may take a third-party change agent to work through the differences involved. Walton (1969) describes how the change agent brings together parties in conflict, creates a balance of power or influence, and helps both parties get their issues out in the open. When this is done, there is a process of mutual accommodation in which each gains some things but gives up others.

Reducing conflicts and stress is a personal issue that at times can be handled alone. Self-change requires understanding the issue, developing a change plan, and enlisting the support of significant others. When this process is too difficult, the change agent is needed to provide direction and support in devising and implementing the change strategy.

# CHAPTER 12

# The Strategy of Adjustment of Expectations

Whenever people come together to combine their efforts to produce results or achieve goals, the possibility of differences or conflicts occurs. People differ in many ways: they have varying experiences, backgrounds, attitudes, personalities, values, goals, and lifestyles. Such differences can erupt into conflicts that erode relationships and make the achievement of goals difficult unless people learn to make appropriate adjustments.

In solving interpersonal conflicts, an analysis of mutual expectations is a key consideration. Expectation analysis allows us to outline and understand more clearly the forms of adjustment that people make when differences occur. It can be argued that every case of interpersonal difference, disruption, or conflict results from the violation of expectations. In cases of organizational conflict, however, other factors such as contrasting or conflicting rules or operational discrepancies must be considered (Molsar and Rogers, 1979). As these researchers point out, conflict between units in an organization can occur when the rules or procedures of one unit are at odds with the others. In this chapter, we are looking at interpersonal conflicts, the difficulties between individuals that may require bringing a change agent or change team into the organization.

## Expectations

Each person enters a relationship with a) certain expectations about his or her own behavior and b) certain expectations about the behavior of the other person. Thus, at least two sets of expectations are involved in every relationship.

The problem that usually arises is that role expectations are at variance with role performance. There is often a difference between what someone else thinks one should do and what one actually does. It is this disparity that creates strain in a relationship. People's differing expectations are the source of most misunderstandings and failures in relationships. If what the boss expects of a subordinate differs from what the subordinate thinks she ought to do, there is a strong possibility that a violation of the boss's expectations will occur, especially if the boss has not spent adequate time in defining his or her expectations to the subordinate. Failure to clarify expectations invariably leads to differences between expectations and performance, as illustrated in the following example:

> Jerry can't understand what is happening. For the past two weeks it seems he can never do anything right. He doesn't know why. His boss, Tim Hartley, is on his back all the time. Jerry is trying to do a good job. He tries to stay out of Mr. Hartley's way and does his own work without bothering anyone. He is expediting his work to prove that he is a good employee who takes the initiative, does not have to rely on the boss for everything, shows results even if others aren't doing a good job. But for some reason that doesn't seem to be enough.

> Tim Hartley is also perplexed. He likes Jerry and considers him a valuable employee. But Jerry is also a problem. Tim thinks to himself, "Why won't he ever check things out before he moves ahead on his own? This would keep me informed and keep him from making unnecessary mistakes. Also, a good employee fits into the team, and he is always working by himself, showing other employees up and creating a lot of resentment."

Here is a clear case of mismatched expectations. Jerry expects himself to behave in certain ways consistent with his definition of a "good" worker. His boss has quite another notion of a good worker and expects Jerry to behave differently than he does now. Unfortunately, neither understands the expectations of the other. One piece of research has shown that in times of changing organizational membership (adding new staff, new leadership coming in from the outside), there is a high probability of mismatched understandings and expectations (Pickhardt, 1981).

## Sanctions

Sanctions, which can be positive or negative, are the rewards or punishments administered to the degree that a person meets or fails to meet expectations. If a subordinate's performance meets the boss's expectations, the boss generally will apply positive sanctions such as praise, recognition, and good will. If the performance violates these expectations, he or she often applies negative sanctions: criticism, withdrawal of trust, or demotions. Tim Hartley, in the case above, is already applying negative sanctions to Jerry.

Human interactions usually move along most smoothly if the following conditions exist:

*1.* The parties interacting have a high level of agreement on expectations of *general* norms, goals, and values.

2. The parties involved agree on mutual role definitions and role expectations. This involves the *specifics* of performance—namely, expectations of *what* is to be done, *when* it is to be done, and *how* it is to be done. In clarifying expectations, attention sometimes is paid only to *what* is expected. However, problems often occur because one's expectations regarding timing—when something is to be done—or performance standards—how it is to be done—are violated.

3. The role performance of one is in agreement with the role expectations of the other, and positive sanctions are the end result of the interaction.

## Points of Conflict at Work

Conflicts in the work situation may arise for the following reasons:

1. The expected norms, goals, and values of the boss are in conflict with those of the subordinate.
2. The role performance of the subordinate does not agree with the expectations of the boss.
3. The role performance of the boss does not agree with the expectations of the subordinate.

In each of the above cases, conflicts may occur when expectations as to what, when, or how the job is to be done are violated, and dissatisfaction with the relationship may result in the direct or indirect application of negative sanctions. A direct sanction could be a reprimand. An indirect sanction could be avoiding another person or cutting back that person's assignment without telling him or her. Feelings of dissatisfaction also may be repressed or hidden or directed toward someone or something else—a process called displacement. The subordinate could displace his frustrations on his wife or family because he may not know how to handle the situation directly.

The case of Tim Hartley and Jerry illustrates what happens when the role performance of the subordinate does not agree with the expectations of the boss. Although Jerry is behaving as consistently as possible with what he considers the requirements of a good subordinate, his performance never will be adequate unless Tim's expectations change. Tim's negative sanctions (criticism, yelling, "being on" Jerry) violate Jerry's expectations about how a boss should behave; Jerry feels that a good boss will not criticize unjustly or without explaining. If Tim continues his pressure, Jerry may react in negative ways. In fact, he is already starting to avoid Tim. This cycle of negative action and reaction can build until a crisis occurs. If open conflict results, the consequence may be the loss of a good employee.

Tim's goals and values, which he has inadequately explained to Jerry, conflict with Jerry's position. Jerry, unaware of the conflict, assumes that he is doing what any reasonable boss would want him to do. If they clarify their expectations, there may not be agreement, but at least both parties would know where change is necessary.

# Interpersonal Adjustment

Assuming that conflicts occur because of a violation of expectations, how does one go about changing the conflict condition? Adjustment is the term often used to describe interpersonal change or an agreement between conflicting parties. From an expectation perspective, what are the adjustment possibilities?

## Possible Methods of Adjustment

For the conflict situation described on page 81, certain kinds of adjustments are possible.

The boss and the subordinate can clarify their norms, goals, or values so that each understands the other's point of view. This of necessity involves mature and extensive communication. To the degree that the disparity is translated into role performance, the following adjustments would be applicable:

1. The subordinate (or boss) can change his or her role performance completely to meet the expectations of the other.
2. The subordinate (or boss) can change his or her expectations completely to coincide with the role performance of the other.
3. There can be a mutual adjustment in which the subordinate alters his or her role performance to a degree, and the boss alters his or her expectations to a similar degree, so that role performance and expectations are compatible. In each of the above cases, the end result is agreement between role performance and expectations.

What are the possible adjustments available to Jerry and his boss? Assuming that one or the other initiates a discussion in which their mismatched expectations are disclosed, and assuming that they want to work out an adjustment, the following are possibilities:

1. Jerry, upon learning of his boss's expectations, could say, "Now that I know what you expect, I'll try to do what you want."
2. Tim Hartley could say, "Jerry I'm glad I found out how you prefer to work. It is a new concept for me, but I think I can accept a new way for a subordinate to work."

3. Each could change. Jerry could agree to keep Tim better informed and to clear plans with him before taking independent action. Tim could agree to give Jerry freedom to work in situations not requiring much team effort and to inform Jerry promptly if things do not go well.

There is another type of adjustment possible. In some cases the two men—recognizing a disparity between role performance and expectations or between general goals or values, and acknowledging that change is difficult or impossible—could "agree to disagree." In such cases, each recognizes and respects the other's position without accepting or adjusting to it. This pattern of agreeing to disagree is not an adjustment in the same sense as those listed above. The "adjustment" comes from the agreement by both persons that a certain area is "out of bounds" as far as the application of sanctions is concerned. There is no change in behavior but some change in expectations: Each now expects that certain subjects will not become issues and that no sanctions will be applied regarding them. This type of adjustment may be possible in certain areas of work life; other areas may be so vital to the relationship that they demand another type of adjustment.

## Some Problems in Adjustment

### Public vs. Private Adjustment

The example of Jerry and Tim emphasizes that public behavior is the essence of adjustment. Complete adjustment is possible only if the change in behavior is accompanied by a positive mental state. If Jerry publicly changes his role performance to meet his boss's expectations, he would appear to have adjusted. Privately, however, he might resent "giving in" and transfer this resentment into other areas.

### The Need for Feedback

Feedback is a necessary element in the process of changing social behavior. It is difficult, if not impossible, for someone to know exactly how he or she is violating the expectations of another if the other does not respond with adequate feedback. Cues may be misread, misinterpreted, or denied if the feedback is not stated clearly in an atmosphere of acceptance. Open communication of expectations and feedback about the degree to which someone has met, or failed to meet, these expectations is sometimes extremely difficult. One may fear that "if I give feedback to him, I may lose what warmth and goodwill we now have," or fear that the other may retaliate. A person likewise may be inhibited from giving feedback by feelings of inadequacy about how to proceed, the lack of an appropriate time, or doubts about being "right" in his or her criticism.

Often, one learns of the expectations of others and how one has or has not met them only via trial and error or in a sudden outburst when someone announces, "I can't take it any longer." Neither of these conditions encourages the mutual sharing of data in the cooperative atmosphere in which feedback is best perceived as helpful to the relationship.

### Adjustment vs. Reconciliation

Adjustment has been discussed in terms of bringing into agreement the behavior of one person with the expectations of another, accompanied by assurances that the modified behavior is acceptable. A phenomenon recognized in many cases of discord is the subsequent process of "reconciliation," which is usually a process of repairing feelings of unity and cohesion.

An examination of a number of case studies (Dyer, 1965) indicates that it is entirely possible for people to be reconciled without achieving any adjustment in the sense described above. A violation of expectations often results in discord and hostility between two people. Afterward, in a moment of mutual sympathy and regret for past actions, they may apologize and then resume a harmonious relationship. But since no modification of either expectation or behavior has occurred, disruption may recur at any time.

It is also possible for adjustment to occur without the attainment of a state of unity. People could meet each other's expectations without feeling good about their behavior. It appears that complete harmony is possible only when both adjustment and reconciliation are achieved.

In terms of reinforcement learning theory, it seems essential that one person's modification of either expectations or behavior is rewarded by the other. One needs to learn not only what one does wrong, but also what one does right. The continuous giving of positive sanctions may be a necessary part of long-term adjustment.

## Implications for Managing Change

This chapter outlines interpersonal conflict and adjustment possibilities in a particular frame of reference. It does not pretend to address the sociopsychological dynamics involved in the difficult process of attitude or behavior change. One should never presume that such adjustments are psychologically easy.

It has been argued that all conflict is a result of one person's behavior not meeting another's expectations, or vice versa. The correction of such conflict is often more complex, for one's behavior and/or expectations may be related to one's "personality," including temperament, conceptions of self, important self-other needs, and the like. Changing role behavior or expectations may demand personal adjustments that are extremely difficult. One's level of maturity also will be a crucial factor in determining one's ability to make adjustments.

The above outline does not suggest which type of conflict is most frequent or which type of adjustment is easiest. Although more research is needed in the area of adjustment, it is commonly believed that it is easier to change one's own expectations than to change another's behavior. For example, it would probably be easier for Tim Hartley to modify his expectations about Jerry than to expect Jerry to change a pattern of activity that has resulted from years of experience, training, and attitudes. However, people in stronger power positions often expect subordinates to change their behavior rather than alter their own expectations.

It should be noted that there are methods available for the *reduction* of conflict in work situations with no actual *adjustment* in the sense defined above; that is, the people involved make some alteration of norms, roles, or role expectations. This avenue generally involves the alteration of the situation that may be fostering certain role behaviors or expectations. For example, if conflict occurs between a boss and a subordinate because the subordinate spends too much time on nonessential matters (thus violating the boss's expectations), a change in job assignment may put the subordinate in an entirely new situation resulting in new, more acceptable behavior. This is one possible solution to the problem between Jerry and Tim—Jerry could be assigned a different boss or a different position in which he could work on his own.

No one should pretend that adjustments are easy, but just discussing expectations sometimes can solve problems almost immediately. In other situations, adjustment will require effort, patience, and understanding as people try to change patterns built up over a lifetime.

Again, those mired in interpersonal conflicts often are unable to devise a useful plan. The intervention of a change agent may be required to identify issues and to work out an adjustment appropriate for all parties involved.

# CHAPTER 13

# Training:
# A Change Strategy

Training programs are important change activities in many organizations and an important tool for change agents. Training directors and specialists are professionals whose job it is to plan and carry out training programs to increase the effectiveness of people at all levels. Because a training program can be time-consuming and expensive without producing results, the nature of effective training must be examined.

*Training,* as presently used, refers to any type of education program that leads to an improvement of performance by a person or persons engaged in an ongoing activity. Underlying the idea of training is the assumption that people can change their behavior.

*Improvement* is generally seen as behavior or performance that is more efficient—producing more output with less expenditure of resources—or more effective—achieving goals with better qualitative or quantitative results. In the case of managers, training in the first sense might make them more efficient; that is, they might be taught to organize their time in such a way that they accomplish the same amount of work more quickly. Alternatively, they might become more effective; that is, they might be taught to handle counseling problems in such a way that people feel better or work more productively after seeing them.

## When to Train People

The question of when to engage in training should be considered seriously. One of our cultural values maintains that everyone can improve, that no one is perfect. Implicit is the notion that everyone could benefit from training concerning every facet of his or her life. Taken to absurd limits, this belief would result in people spending all their time being trained. Realistically, the question is whether there is some level of performance (either a minimum level or an optimum level) that people should achieve. If they have not reached this level, should some type of training be instigated?

Often, those responsible for training decisions have not thought through what levels or limits must be reached but nevertheless persist in initiating all kinds of training programs. Moreover, most training programs include little or no evaluation to determine if the training has accomplished its proposed goals.

If realistic performance levels have been established, however, and if people have not achieved these levels, some type of training might be appropriate.

Training is necessary as a means of improving performance when a person is inexperienced in the role or job demands. Thus, new employees often go through a training program to prepare them to perform their jobs at the required level.

## When Not to Train People

Despite the cultural value that anyone can improve, training should not be utilized when:

1. The time taken for the training program would not be worth the benefits that would accrue.
2. The beneficial results of the training program are questionable in terms of the expenditures of resources.
3. The training program would result in behavior change that is not functional or useful to the goals of the organization.
4. More effective results can be achieved by simpler (less time-consuming, less costly) methods. In a managers' program, we might try to train all managers in the art of counseling when it actually would be simpler to refer people with problems to a professional. Of course, provision would have to be made for trained counselors on an organizational basis.
5. The reasons for inadequate performance are location, low motivation, or organizational constraints. Under those conditions, training will not improve the performance level; what is needed is intervention at a different level in the organization. It has been suggested that the following question be asked: "If the employee's life depended on it, could he or she perform the desired behavior at the desired level?" If the answer is no, then training is needed. If the answer is yes, it is not a training matter. Other factors reducing performance must be addressed.

## Types of Training Programs

In attempts to bring about an improvement of performance, the following actions commonly are taken.

## Cognitive Learning Activities

The hope here is that people reading or listening to descriptions of new ways of behaving will understand them well enough and be sufficiently motivated to try out the new behaviors. The problems with this method include communication, comprehension, skill competency, and motivation. It is hard to determine whether people reading or hearing material understand it the way the author intended. It is even more difficult to know whether they are capable of putting into action the kind of performance specified. This inherently weak activity must be supported so people will understand what is presented and develop the necessary skills. Skill-practice exercises or cases can help expand cognitive material.

## Training Meetings, Programs, Conferences

There are a wide variety of formats for training programs. The most limited merely bring people together and tell them in a variety of ways (lectures, films, tapes, handout materials) what they should be doing.

The better programs do the following:

1. Allow people to talk about and explore the reasons for their current performance.
2. Allow them to set goals for improved performance.
3. Allow them to practice new ways of behaving.
4. Provide feedback on the effectiveness of new behaviors.

All programs, both good and bad, involve the problem of learning transfer. Whenever we take people off the job to train them in a program setting, we confront the fact that when they return to their jobs they may revert to old ways of behaving. A good deal of research has indicated that people need support and reinforcement in the ongoing situation in order to be successful in trying and continuing new behaviors. Training is best done in the actual work setting so that transfer problems are eliminated. This raises the issue of whether training is best accomplished as an individual or group effort. Some skills may be essentially individual (such as handling a computer) and some are collective in nature (such as improving shared decision-making skills). Either way, they are best learned in the context of the ongoing support of the work social system.

## Coaching

Coaching, an old principle of training, derives from the work of the athletic coach, who watches his players practice, assesses their performance during a game, takes people out of the game, gives them instructions, and then puts them back. Afterward there is a critique of performance, more practice, and another game.

This old principle is losing ground because in many situations it is awkward to have a coach present. Even so, many organizations are experimenting with coaching; some are assigning new people to experienced older managers who act as coaches or mentors for a period of training. A major activity for an effective manager is coaching subordinates. Boss (1983) has described the use of a regular personal management interview (PMI) in which a range of issues are discussed, including the opportunity for coaching. Boss presents clear evidence that a regular interview maintains the gains that comes from team training.

## Consultants

One type of coach is the consultant, who usually comes from outside the unit; watches the ongoing performance; and then gives instruction, guidance, directions, and practice sessions in an attempt to improve the performance level. (Schein, 1969) has described process consultation as the consultant helping the client examine and improve processes on the job.

## Job Rotation

One form of training is job rotation, in which a person spends time in a variety of jobs to gain specific first-hand experience, often with coaching by a qualified person.

## Modeling

Recently, many training programs have employed a modeling format. The usual practice is to videotape either an actual performance or an enacted scene to demonstrate desired or undesirable behaviors. Trainees practice via role-playing the behaviors they have observed. Poras and Andersen (1981), who describe the use of modeling in an industrial setting, have evidence that improved performance results.

# Qualities of a Good Training Program

Having examined various aspects of training and training programs, we can isolate the processes usually found to be effective.

## Examination of Performance

An effective training program includes an opportunity for trainees to examine their current performance level in such a way that they understand what is effective and what needs improving. An important aspect of this process is feedback—data from others as to how they are doing in the job. A weakness of many training programs is that trainees often are uncertain of how to improve; there has been little or no collection of data about their performance. Currently, many training programs begin with feedback on back-home job performance collected for each participant prior to the training, thus, training can focus on real performance needs. This feedback, collected from one's boss, peers, and subordinates, differs from feedback given in the training setting from people who are strangers (Dyer, 1983).

## Establishment of Change Goals

To improve one's performance, one must know what one is currently doing and decide upon goals for improvement. To make such a decision, one must know one's own potentials and limitations. To be truly motivated, one must make personal commitments. Motivation and commitment are weaker if someone else establishes the change goals and the worker is not involved in the change process.

## New Information, Ideas, Principles, Directions

Once one understands the need for improvement and has set goals, one can employ new ideas, new directions, and new principles. Until the first two conditions have been met, it is hard to know whether one really needs new information or how to use it after one gets it. Too many programs consist of funneling new information to people before they have any feel for how to apply it effectively to their personal situations.

## Experimentation and Practice

People do not change easily or all at once. Most of us need a chance to try out new ways and to become familiar with new procedures. Too often, training programs do not build in such experimentation and practice. In training meetings or workshops away from the actual work situation, there is no opportunity to try out new ways of behaving on the job. The presumption is that trainees will have enough courage and insight to return to work and implement new behavior that has not previously been used in that setting. Certain training activities that allow people to practice new behavior include role-playing, exercises, games, and unstructured situations such as the T-group or experimental group.

## Climate

The appropriate climate is essential for trainees to feel free to experiment with new behaviors and to be receptive to feedback. If the climate is threatening and one feels he or she is being criticized or evaluated negatively or will be mocked for making a mistake, one will be reluctant to change one's behavior.

The optimum conditions are most advantageous when combined in the immediate work setting. If conditions can be modified to create the right climate, if people can examine their own performance under the supervision of a coach, superior, or consultant, and if these conditions continue, an employee may maintain new ways of behaving.

## Follow-up

Once a program of improvement is established, a follow-up—essentially a continuation of the training conditions—is important. Periodically, the person in training should examine his or her performance, receive more feedback data, gain new information, and then try again. If this process can be built into general work activities, all employees will be constantly working on their own improvement.

## Organization Support

Too often, training programs fail because trainees returning to their jobs are not supported in new activities suggested by the training. New behavior must be encouraged and supported by superiors, peers, and subordinates. Team-training—the training of a total work unit—is one way to ensure that training is utilized in the organization. If one's superior supports the training program, he or she can lend organizational support by rewarding the new behaviors through regular organization channels. It also reinforces new behaviors if the reward system supports the new actions quickly and directly. Informal rewards (praise, commendation, pats on the back) can be given immediately even though formal rewards such as a raise or promotion come later.

Conversely, a major block to improved performance is erected when the superior is not aware of the training and does not recognize, encourage, or reward the new behavior.

# Common Issues in Training

In planning any training program, a common set of issues usually must be addressed:

*1. Who should be invited to a training program?* Attendance at a training program held at a recreation site is often seen as a company reward rather than a serious effort to improve performance. Participants should attend training programs only if they feel a *need* to improve their performance. While it is possible to deal with people who do not want to be at the training program or are there for the wrong reasons, it is clearly more effective if they attend voluntarily because they feel a need for the training.

**2.** *How long should training programs last?* There is no established time frame. In fact, one of the stumbling blocks to improved performance is that training is seen as a three-day or five-day event rather than an ongoing process. Although effective training programs can be held a half a day per week over several weeks, it has been observed that a certain amount of start-up time is necessary to get people involved in the learning process. Programs that last over a longer, continuous period avoid the loss of time experienced in stopping and starting.

**3.** *Where should training be held?* There is a rationale for conducting training away from the job setting so learning can take place without interruptions. But there is also a rationale for training directly in the work situation to avoid transfer problems. The latter appears to be more practical in terms of time, costs, and schedules. It is not necessarily more effective.

**4.** *Who should conduct training activities?* Training should be a management function. The best training probably is some form of direct coaching from superior to subordinate. Consultants and training specialists can be used, but only as a support to the manager. Even in more formal training programs, it is possible to prepare line managers to conduct training sessions (Dyer, 1983). However, there is evidence that participants appreciate the stimulation created by special resource people; a training staff of these resource people plus managers may provide the most useful mix. The danger is that members of the organization may regard training as a staff function separate from the real work people do.

## Implications for Managing Change

Training, in the sense that people in organizations try to improve the performance of other people through some type of learning experience, is probably a basic process in any system, particularly at the informal level. Formal training programs that command a large expenditure of resources are a relatively recent phenomenon. Because many organizations do use training as a major change activity, managers should evaluate these programs carefully and take measures to determine if the training produces the desired results. Training in the sense of on-the-job coaching should be built into the manager's role, and the competent manager-coach should be identified and rewarded.

# CHAPTER 14

# Planning Individual Change*

"I wish I could change." How many times have you told yourself that and then done nothing about it? It may be that you didn't have the desire, time, or, possibly, even the ability to change. Besides, it is easier to wish than to work.

Your ability to be successful in making a change is determined, to a large extent, on how you answer these three questions. First, do you truly want to change? Are you sufficiently motivated to get yourself started and maintain a change effort? Second, do you have enough time to put into this effort? Third, do you have the ability to make the desired change?

Ask yourself why you want to make the change. Is it something you consider good for yourself? Or is it something that others think is good for you? If you perceive a discrepancy between the way you are and the way you would like to be, you have *some* motivation to change. Obviously, the greater the discrepancy, the greater the motivation. For many people, the discrepancy is so miminal that their attitude reflects, "I can live with what I have." Although there may be many reasons for making a change, in the final analysis the question remains, "How badly do you want to change?"

How much time do you have to put into a change effort? Usually people want a "quick fix" so they can get on with their lives. But when it comes to a long-term behavior change, there are no quick fixes. Change takes time. When you consider the amount of time needed to learn, practice, and apply new behavior, you realize it is not a short-term effort. One manager wanted to become more connected with his employees; his goal was to go out to lunch with them and to interact freely. It was only after six months of concentrated effort that he was able to say that he had succeeded.

People doubt that an old dog can learn new tricks. Is it possible to change as one gets older? Obviously there are some areas in which it is extremely difficult or even impossible to change: It is unlikely that one can grow taller, become smarter, become an expert without training, or change one's basic personality. In most other cases, however, people can

---

* This chapter written by Robert D. Dyer.

and do make changes—in fact, they learn, grow, develop, and make changes all their lives. Many older individuals are exploring second career opportunities because they are anxious to learn and want to make the changes necessary to remain productive members of society.

The example of Terri Wallen illustrates the dynamics of change:

> Terri is a perfectionist. She is convinced that this got her where she is—vice-president of commercial loans, the highest level a woman has achieved in her company. Her perfectionism resulted in perfect work—not only from her but also from her employees. She reviewed everything that went out of her department and made sure it met her standards. She knows, though, that unless she makes some changes, she will be inundated with work. In her new position, she will have to delegate work to people whose standards may not be as exacting as hers.

Terri finds it extremely difficult even to consider changing her drive for perfection. It is a trait that has been rewarded all through her life. She was a straight-A student, received many honors for her work, and was routinely described as a "bright, capable girl." She does not want to give that up. Even though she feels she must make some changes, she isn't sure the rewards will be worth the effort. For Terri, change will be more difficult than for someone whose behavior pattern has not been successful for some time.

# A Plan for Individual Change

Making a behavior change is difficult and sometimes frightening. The difficult part is learning new skills and applying them, especially in stressful situations. The frightening aspect is uncertainty that the change actually will provide the anticipated rewards.

Change is work. It is not easy to alter old, ingrained habits that served well in the past. An effective change effort requires a well-planned program that is implemented in a systematic manner. The following principles are crucial to success: First, the change effort should be *goal-directed*. Goals should be specific, realistic and measurable. Second, you must understand your *motivation* for making the change. Certain motivational factors, either internal or external to the individual, help or hinder the change effort. Third, you must *practice* the new behavior. Fourth, you should focus on *minimum behavior change* rather than on personality or "style" changes; the more you focus on small behavior changes, the greater your chances for success. Fifth, the change effort should be *supported by significant others*. Many people who try to make changes on their own may regard asking for help as a sign of weakness. They are wrong. One reason Alcoholics Anonymous and other such groups are successful is that they provide support to individuals making changes, especially in times of stress. Finally, your program should be designed to *maintain the change achieved*.

Let us review each of these basic change conditions.

## Goal-Setting

All behavior is goal-directed. Too often, people are involved in activities that keep them busy but do not lead to the accomplishment of their most important objectives. Goal-directed behavior that is efficient and effective promises a greater chance for success, but only if the goals set are the relevant ones.

Goals should be specific, realistic and measurable. Specific goals address a single behavior, number, unit of time, etc. For example, "to improve my interpersonal skills" is a fuzzy general goal. A specific goal in the same area would be "to start calling each subordinate by his or her first name." Realistic goals are those that are possible to achieve. Goals should not be so difficult you know you can't reach them or so easy that little or no effort is required to accomplish them. A realistic goal for an indecisive man might be to "start making immediate decisions at home." When his wife asks "What do you want for dinner?" he could state his choice instead of saying, "I don't know—anything you want." All goals should be measurable so you know when you have achieved something; when possible, obtain "hard" data to show yourself that you have done what you said you were going to do. If your goal is to improve communications by holding regular one-on-one meetings with subordinates, your schedule book should indicate the meetings held.

## Motivation

Motivation occurs when an individual experiences a state of dissatisfaction, or "hurts" for something he or she doesn't have, and acts in order to remedy the situation. If the person doesn't "hurt" enough, he or she won't put forth the effort to change. If the person hurts too much, he or she may become paralyzed and, consequently, unable even to consider making the change. It is essential to reach a state of "creative tension" sufficient to result in appropriate motivation to make a change.

There are many reasons for making changes or not making changes. It's an individual matter. What motivates one person may not motivate another. Each of us must identify the "payoff" for making the change as well as the factors "blocking" us from changing. Being *aware* of these factors is the first step in making a change. Until one says, "I can't stand this in myself any longer; I have got to change," one's motivation is insufficient.

## Practice Time

In sports there is time for practice; in school there is "lab" time; but at work there is little, if any, time for practice—an individual's training is "on-the-job." In exercises at the end of this chapter, you have the opportunity to "practice" your new behavior, both behaviorally and mentally.

## Minimum Behavior Change

Rather than trying to achieve your specific objective immediately, according to this plan you will first try your new behavior in a situation in which there is a low risk of failing and a high probability of succeeding. Then you will move *gradually* into more "risky" situations until you have achieved your specific objective. Here are some examples of minimum, low-risk changes:

> **Assertiveness:** At home, make decisions about meals or TV programs.
>
> With friends, make decisions about a movie or restaurant to visit.
>
> **Interpersonal Competence:** Spend 30 seconds with a particular subordinate.
>
> Take a coffee break with a subordinate.
>
> **Listening:** Ask wife, child, subordinate: "What is the one thing that has bothered you most this week?" Listen and write down the response.

In Exercise D at the end of this chapter, you will start by identifying a low-risk situation in which you can apply your new behavior. Then you will identify other situations in which you can "practice" your new behavior until you feel ready to work on your specific objective. For each situation, you are to identify the "what, how, who, and when." The following definitions may help you in your planning.

> **What:** What is your goal (general and specific)? What is your payoff for achieving your goal? What are your chances for success in your effort? How will you know if you have succeeded?
>
> **Who:** Who will be involved? Who will help you plan your strategy for making the change? Who will help you when things aren't going right?
>
> **How:** What are you going to do? How are you going to do it? Be as specific as you can in identifying how you will perform your new behavior. Have contingency plans ready.
>
> **When:** When will you start your new behavior? Is there a time when conditions are best? Set a time for review and a time when you should be finished.

## Maintaining Behavioral Change

Once a change effort has been started, it is important to maintain it. Most people experience a letdown or a failure along the way. It is necessary to cope with these experiences effectively so you don't lose ground, i.e., for every step forward you take two steps backward. Once they encounter failure many people give up their program totally. There are three ways to deal with discouragement and proceed. First, identify those who will support you in your efforts. People who attempt changes by themselves often fail in their efforts, whereas those with a support system are more successful. Second, identify the potential blocks to making your change. These blocks come in subtle forms; for example, "I have too much to do," "I don't have enough time," "I forgot." If you can anticipate blocks, you are more effective in overcoming them. Third, reserve time for reviewing your efforts. Use your support system to discuss your activities, how you feel about your progress, etc. These reviews will help you maintain perspective.

## Support Systems

Support systems are people who will help you in your change effort with encouragement and feedback. They should know what you are going to do and how you are going to do it; if possible, they should see you try your new behavior. You must trust these people to be honest and supportive in working with you.

## Blocks

As you proceed in your change effort, you may encounter blocks that hinder your chances for success. It is important to identify these blocks before they become reasons or excuses for not making the change. One manager who was trying to become more decisive found great resistance from his staff, who liked his "old style" better because they could avoid responsibilities more easily. Blocks may be internal or external to the individual. To review some of the potential blocks, look at Exercise B.

## Review

An important part of the change process is review time, in which you periodically sit back and assess your progress. You should review your goal—is it still realistic and challenging? Are you able to measure any progress? Has your support system given any feedback? Are any changes needed in your strategy? Review sessions should occur often enough that you can benefit from feedback. If you wait too long, you may be wasting time and energy on an ineffective effort.

## Goal Setting

Returning to our example of Terri Wallen, let's examine how she dealt with her "perfectionism":

> Terri decided to focus on the aspect of her perfectionism that she felt was creating the most problems for her. Her goal was to reduce her reviews of subordinates' work in order to give the subordinates more freedom. There would be a double payoff: She would do less work and her people would have more control over their work. This should increase their motivation for doing a good job. In other areas she would continue "making sure they give their best effort."

If Terri could give up some control and give her subordinates more autonomy, she could reduce the negative impact of her perfectionism on herself and her employees.

## Minimum Behavior Change

Terri Wallen's change effort actually started at home, where she always monitored her child's homework, making sure it was done perfectly. She decided to work out a contract with her daughter, according to which Terri would not review the homework but would help if necessary when the homework was returned. Both mother and child survived beautifully.

## Maintain Behavior Change

Terri developed two support systems. At home, her husband was more than happy to support her in her change effort. They discussed her plans and developed strategies for feedback sessions and review times. At work, her boss became her support system. He was able to watch her operate in staff meetings and gave her feedback on what he observed. Most of the blocks that Terri identified were internal—her fears of not doing a perfect job, of failure, and of not being recognized as a competent manager.

## Implications for Managing Change

There is considerable evidence that a person who wants to achieve real change in a specific area must make a strong, concerted effort to make it happen. Change means work. This chapter has outlined some of the work involved in planning a specific change in one's behavior. One sign that a person is motivated to work on a personal change program is when he or she begins to work on the activities suggested in this chapter.

# Exercises for Creating Change

## Exercise A: Goal-Setting Activities

In planning change, consider both a "general" goal (i.e., "I want to be a better listener") and a "specific" goal (i.e., "I want to be a better listener with my boss").

General Goal: _____

_____

_____

_____

Specific Goal: _____

_____

_____

_____

Describe present behavior that indicates you are not doing what you would like to be doing (i.e., "When my boss talks to me, I think of rebuttals to his statements rather than listen to what he is saying").

_____

_____

_____

_____

How will you measure the accomplishment of your specific goal? (i.e., "I am able to paraphrase, to my boss's satisfaction, what he or she has said to me.") List two ways.

_____

_____

_____

_____

Is your goal realistic? (An example of an unrealistic goal is "I am going to stop being an autocratic manager.") Describe how your goal is challenging, yet not so hard it would take unusual effort to achieve, or so easy it requires no effort.

_____

_____

_____

## Exercise B: Motivation Activity

The two lists below show some of the reasons people make a change (payoffs) or don't make a change (blocks). Read through the lists and identify those reasons that affect you.

| *"Blocks"* | *"Payoffs"* |
|---|---|
| Fear of the unknown | Greater recognition |
| Complacency | More freedom |
| Fear of failure | Sense of achievement |
| Lack of skill | More productive |
| Takes too much time | More efficient |
| Don't want more responsibility | More responsibility |
| Don't see the need for change | Increase feeling of self-worth |
| Too much effort required | Be of help to others |
| Fear of rejection | Better interpersonal relationships |
| Forced to make the change | More control over what you are |
| Old habits | doing |
| (Other) | (Other) |

Which of the "blocks" affect you the most? Rank the top three.

*1.* _____

*2.* _____

*3.* _____

In what ways can you reduce the impact of these blocks? What can you do to cope with these blocks so they don't prevent you from initiating your change effort?

_____

_____

_____

_____

What is the "pay-off" for making your change? Identify what you will get for making the change. Be as specific as possible.

_____

_____

_____

_____

In making a change, one gives up something. You may give up "old habits," comfort, predictability, guaranteed rewards, etc. Change is moving from the known to the unknown. What will you be giving up in starting your change process?

_____

_____

_____

_____

_____

On a scale from 1 to 7, assess the strength of your motivation to change your behavior.

     1(low)     2     3     4     5     6     7(high)

If your rating is on the low side (4 or less), what can you do to increase your motivation? How can you increase your "payoff?"

_____

_____

_____

_____

## Exercise C: Practice Session

_Mental Image:_ Imagine the situation in which the new behavior will be tried. Who will be involved? How will you behave? Where will it take place? What will you do if you encounter resistance? Think of two to three different ways you might handle this situation. Write down your thoughts (how you feel; how you think you will behave; how you think others will behave in a particular situation; etc.) What things made you feel uncomfortable with the new behavior? How can you cope with them? What did you like about your new behavior?

_Role-Play:_ Find a partner (spouse, colleague, friend, etc.) to whom you can describe the situation and what you want to accomplish. Have your partner take a role—for example, your demanding boss—and then act out how you would handle the problem. Try several different approaches and get feedback from your partner on how he or she felt about your behavior.

*Script-Writing:* Write out the situation as you perceive it. Describe what you would do and how you would do it. Again, be as specific as possible. Develop as many alternative approaches as you can.

*Video-Tape:* If you have a video recorder, either at home or at work, you might role-play or rehearse your new behavior and record it. Try a variety of behaviors to see what works best for you.

## Exercise D: Minimum Behavior Change Activities

*First Situation* (Low-risk, easy, high probability for success)

*1.* What is your goal? What is your payoff?

_____

_____

_____

_____

_____

*2.* Who is to be involved?

_____

_____

_____

_____

*3.* How are you going to do it?

_____

_____

_____

_____

_____

*4.* When will you do it?

_____

_____

_____

_____

5. Alternate plans:
   a. How will you deal with unexpected reactions?
   b. What did you do well in your change effort?
   c. What would you change?

_____

_____

_____

_____

_____

**Second Situation** (More risky, a little more difficult, still a good chance for success)

1. What is your goal? What is your payoff?

_____

_____

_____

_____

_____

2. Who is to be involved?

_____

_____

_____

3. How are you going to do it?

_____

_____

_____

_____

_____

4. When will you do it?

_____

_____

_____

_____

5. Alternate plans:
   *a.* How will you deal with unexpected reactions?
   *b.* What did you do well in your change effort?
   *c.* What would you change?

_____

_____

_____

_____

_____


***Third Situation*** (even more risky, more difficult, not sure of what will happen)

*1.* What is your goal? What is your payoff?

_____

_____

_____

_____


*2.* Who is to be involved?

_____

_____

_____

_____


*3.* How are you going to do it?

_____

_____

_____

_____

_____


*4.* When will you do it?

_____

_____

_____

_____

5. Alternate plans:
   *a.* How will you deal with unexpected reactions?
   *b.* What did you do well in your change effort?
   *c.* What would you change?

_____

_____

_____

_____

_____

_____

## Exercise E: Maintaining Behavioral Change

*Support System:* Who will support you in your change effort?

_____

_____

_____

_____

How will you use your support system?

Planning: _____

Review: _____

Feedback: _____

Other: _____

*Blocks:* What will block you in your attempts to change?

*External:*
1. Expectations of others (boss, peers, etc.)
2. Work piling up
3. Not enough time
4. No support from boss
5. Other

*Internal:* (Go back to Exercise A and identify your feelings about changing. How are you coping with them?

_____

_____

_____

*Review:* Identify times for meeting with your support system to start your program, get feedback, and review your progress.

Times: Start _____

Feedback _____

Review _____

# SECTION THREE

# Group and Organizational Change

## Introduction

A strategy for trying to alter the output of a group or the collective behavior of people in an organization will undoubtedly differ from a plan for changing an individual. For one thing, groups and organizations develop cultural patterns—ways of thinking and acting that everyone accepts as "the way things are done around here." These patterns persist through time, and a change in perform-ance may require looking at the organization's culture and devising a plan to change it.

In the group or unit, the focus of the change strategy may be on altering certain group practices or building a commitment to working together to achieve common goals. Team building is one strategy for getting a total group to plan some changes together.

All organizations involve a complex of connected sub-systems (social, technical and administrative) as well as an open interaction with the external environment. When we think about changing the outputs of an organization it is critical to see which parts of the organization are mostly connected with the area of change. It is vital to the success of an organizational change program that a good diagnosis of the total system be achieved before a plan of action is devised. Diagnosis before action is always the watch word.

This section considers ways of diagnosing groups and organizations by looking at cultural patterns, system elements, and group processes. Following the diagnosis, a plan of team building, culture change, or organization development can then be put into action.

# CHAPTER 15

# Cultural Barriers to Participative Change

The early studies and experiments involving planned change (Hawthorne studies, Lewin studies, Coch–French studies) all emphasize collective participation and support in the change endeavor. Although change can and does occur at the individual and larger collectivity levels, the use of group participation as a change mechanism is certainly vital for the change agent to understand.

It is equally important to recognize that our society comprises certain cultural conditions that militate against people working together and supporting one another as change occurs. Unless the change agent understands these barriers, change programs could be blocked. In contrast, taking these factors into account may lead to a strategy with a greater chance for success.

It should be noted that different groups, organizations, sections of the country, and social-status levels may exhibit the barrier characteristics to differing degrees. The data-gathering process should specify the presence and intensity of such factors so they can be incorporated in the action planning.

## Barrier One: Attitudes Toward Minority Groups

The issue of equality of opportunity for women, blacks, Hispanics, older people, and other factions or minority groups has received a great deal of attention in the courts. Despite important gains in equality of opportunity, serious forms of conscious or unconscious discrimination still exist and could affect any shared decision-making, goal-setting, or planning. The majority faction could, either consciously or unconsciously, discriminate against minorities in the interaction process. The minority people might be ignored, rebuffed, put down, pigeonholed into certain stereotyped responses or positions, and in various ways made to feel left out. The end result could be a silent, uncommitted minority who do not really support the prospective change and either drag their feet or actually oppose the majority.

If issues of fairness and equity for minority groups have not been resolved in an organization, they may occupy such a central position in people's priorities that other change issues may command little attention. One of the problems associated with this barrier is that those who form the majority often are unaware of their own biases and behavior that create problems for others.

## Barrier Two: Assumed Superiority

It appears to be rather natural to accord prestige, deference, and authority to those who have acquired more of certain items that are held in esteem in our culture. We tend to look up to individuals who have greater experience, age, education, money, and/or social position. Not only do many people lacking in these areas feel inadequate to talk on an equal basis with the more favorably endowed, but they also feel that the latter have a natural right to occupy positions of dominance. They may consider it presumptuous of themselves to question, criticize, or comment. Then, too, many higher-status people agree that they should be accorded more prestige and authority.

Some people are able to make a superior contribution in certain areas because of a higher degree of competence. However, one person is seldom, if ever, superior in all areas, and there is no reason why he or she should be constantly accorded or should assume positions of authority. Some claim positions of dominance because of greater age, and our cultural patterns support this idea of respect and deference both to parents and to other older people. On the other hand; those with wealth or social position often are accorded higher status than is warranted by their objectively considered competency, knowledge, or skills. Feelings of superiority or inferiority are real blocks to effective participation.

When assumed superiority infects a situation, the change process can be severely damaged. Those with the higher assumed status may push for changes that those of lower status do not really want or support but with which they are fearful or reluctant to disagree openly. The "superior" persons assume that the others are committed to a change plan when in fact a false consensus may prevail. This means that people agree publicly, but privately they may disagree and find ways to sabotage the change efforts.

## Barrier Three: Formal Status

Closely allied to barrier two is the formal status hierarchy found in organizations such as business, schools, churches, and government agencies. Many have a division of labor and authority ranked very precisely

in terms of offices ranging from president on down to supervisors, foremen, and finally workers or lay members.

When people of varying ranks are involved in change programs, those in the lower positions often feel a great reluctance to participate as equals. A second lieutenant does not easily criticize the ideas of the base commander, nor does a file clerk or bank teller feel free to openly discuss his or her views of the company's needs with the president. The feeling that one's job may be in jeopardy if one violates the rules or expectations of the higher-status person reduces many people to the role of "yes-men." The reverse also occurs—a higher-status person may unconsciously resent the participation of a lower-ranking person. He or she might perceive this participation as a threat to his or her own position or assume that those in authority over him disapprove of such action. It is a common experience for those higher in the organization to be committed to a change plan that is resisted by lower-level people who have become skilled in hiding their feelings from those in authority over them.

# Barrier Four: Overdependence on the Leader

When a group or unit in an organization considers creating change, a barrier occurs where the formal leader is dominant and others become overly dependent. Dependency is one way of reducing the threat of an authority figure; if one always agrees with the leader and does exactly what is wanted, then one can feel safe from criticism, reprimand, or loss of rewards.

In an early study on leadership by Lippitt and White, the researchers created work units in a boys' club. Some of the boys functioned under a democratic leader, some under an authoritarian leader, and some under a laissez-faire leader who was permissive and let them do anything they wanted. Activity was poorest under the laissez-faire leader and best under the democratic leader.

These studies also showed that when the authoritarian leader was absent, little action was taken by subordinates. Also, the interaction that took place was predominantly between leader and individual members; subordinates tended not to learn to work together. Under the democratic leader there was less dependency, and the boys continued to work even when the leader was not present.

High dependency on the leader can result in change if the leader is strongly and consistently involved. There is evidence that in certain situations dependency can shift to counterdependency as some of the subordinates tire of the continual dominance of the leader and individually or collectively begin to rebel against or actively resist the influence of the leader.

# Barrier Five: Institutionalized Cynicism

A common reaction to suggestions that a group or organization plan to improve is the cynical response that "You can't get things changed around here. We've tried things like this before and they don't work." When statements like this are made and there is a general nodding of heads, there is a shared feeling, called "institutionalized cynicism," that change is not possible.

Yankelovich (1981) who has been gathering information about attitudes toward business for many years, has shown that cynicism about one's work is pervasive in our society. In 1966, only 26 percent of the population agreed with the statement "People running the country don't care what happens to people like me." Ten years later, in 1977, 60 percent of the people agreed.

In 1970, 21 percent of the people believed that "Next year will be worse than this year." By 1980, the number agreeing with this statement had increased to 55 percent. Many people just do not feel that change can come about that will make a difference for them.

Along with this general cynicism regarding improvement, there is even more pessimism about the role of government. In less than two decades, confidence in those running the government dropped from 69 percent to 29 percent, and feelings that government is run for the benefit of the few rather than the many rose from 28 percent to 65 percent.

If cynicism is pervasive in an organization, it presents a most formidable barrier toward the achievement of change.

# Barrier Six: Pseudo-Acceptance

A major block to change programs is the common tendency to pretend to be enthusiastic and supportive of change plans. Chapter 22 on dysfunctional agreement examines one aspect of this in greater detail.

Some people feel it is a mark of a poor employee to disagree with assumed preferences of the boss or the majority. In change programs, this pseudo-acceptance creates difficulties in sustaining action when the commitment level of people involved is really nonexistent.

# Implications for Managing Change

There is no easy solution for reducing or removing any of the above-named barriers that can block change efforts. But when change programs involve a number of people and success is determined to some extent by their active participation, any blockage to effective involvement or commitment must be considered. This chapter points out some of the per-

vasive conditions that hinder changes. Later chapters in this section will look at strategies that promise to reduce these barriers.

Instead of a pat solution, what can be offered is the recommendation of a process. First, any program of planned change should start from the premise that one or more barriers may be present in the system. It therefore would be wise to investigate this possibility in the data-gathering phase of a change program. People could be asked directly if they are aware of any of these barriers in themselves and in others.

Should the data indicate the presence of major problems that could hinder the change effort, it may be expedient to hold the original change issue in abeyance and concentrate on the removal or reduction of the resistant force.

All these resistance factors represent sensitive, deep-rooted, often emotionally laden concerns. Programs exist for confronting people in organizations about issues of discrimination and prejudice. False assumptions or ineffective attitudes or behavior also can be identified and raised to the level of consciousness so that people can consider alternative ways of behavior. When the barrier issue is identified and discussed, it might seem inadvisable or inopportune to tackle it directly at that time. With this information out in the open, it may be possible to clearly circumvent the barrier and continue with the original change proposal. The process identified here is designed to uncover barriers if they exist and raise them to the level of consciousness so that the action described in later chapters can be appropriately considered and taken.

# CHAPTER 16

# Group Dynamics and Team Building: A Vehicle for Change

A hard-core fact of our organizational world is that most activities in which we engage occur within the context of a functioning group. People are either working with others on projects or doing work that is part of a group or unit activity. There is ample evidence that most organizations are composed of interlocking groups or departments; therefore, an important skill for managers or change agents is handling groups, not just individuals. Within organizations, change is usually achieved by utilizing the powerful forces operating in work groups.

## The Group as a Vehicle for Change

The study of group dynamics has consistently shown that individuals are strongly influenced by other members of groups to which they belong. Group members can exert powerful pressures, in various ways, to shape and channel the behaviors of others who are a part of the unit. Early studies by social psychologists Sherif and Ashe clearly demonstrated that many people assigned to be part of a temporary experimental group will change their own perceptions and judgments in order to agree with the majority opinion. In the Ashe experiments, naive subjects were put into experimental groups with people who were all confederates of the experimenter. All group members were shown two black lines on a white background and asked which of the two lines was longer. One was, in fact, somewhat longer than the other. The naive subjects, who were last to report, heard everyone else maintain that what to them seemed to be the shorter line was the longer of the two. When their turn came, a large number of the naive subjects denied their own perceptions and said the shorter line was longer in order to avoid being different from the others. Sherif's experiments used a different vehicle but showed the same results.

Not only has research like the Ashe studies demonstrated the power of group influence, but direct field examinations in ongoing work units have shown similar trends. Starting with the earlier Hawthorne research, any number of studies have indicated that work performance can be strongly influenced by the attitudes and performance of group members. In the areas of training and development, groups have been widely used to help people learn new behaviors. From 1950 to 1970, the training group (T-group) was perhaps the primary vehicle for management development, and group membership and influence were predominant forces in the learning process. Out of much of this activity emerged the process widely known as "team-building." Because people live and work in groups, procedures were developed to help individuals develop better teamlike interactions and relationships in order to achieve goals.

Most managers work with a collection of individuals who must interact, decide, plan, share, communicate, and help each other to some degree. Thus, it is important for managers to understand the dimensions of group life that clearly influence the behavior of the group member. An understanding of these factors may help the manager identify problem areas, places where change in group action can be effected, and ways that group activity can be important in achieving change. Anyone who desires to accomplish change must be able to tap into the important forces operating in a group. What are these forces?

## Group Norms

Every group arrives at a set of formal and/or informal standards or norms that identify for the group member what kinds of behaviors are expected. At the same time, the permissible degree of variance or deviance from the norm is also established. It is interesting that in many groups the norms that define behavior have never been discussed, let alone written or voted on. Similarly, most families maintain a wide range of unwritten, undiscussed, but clearly understood standards. For example, most families have never discussed the "incest taboo," the prohibition against sexual contact between members of the same family, but they nevertheless understand and obey it.

One of the early discoveries made by the Hawthorne studies was the power of group norms. In an effort to determine if worker performance could be enhanced by a monetary incentive, one group of workers was offered a bonus if they would increase their output. Nothing happened. Production stayed at the same level whether incentives were added or taken away. When a researcher asked the workers why they did not respond to the incentive, he was told that the group had decided it was not to their advantage to increase production. If they produced more, they reasoned, one of two negative things would result—management either would raise the required output or would find that the increased output decreased the number of workers needed. Hence, the group norm evolved stipulating that no one would produce more than the group standard. Informal group rewards and punishments were applied to ensure compliance.

Some group standards may be regarded as contrary to the needs of the organization or management, while others contribute to the formal organization. In one manufacturing company, the norm allowed workers to take as long as they needed on their rest breaks. The occasional lengthy rest periods that resulted could be interpreted as contrary to the best interests of the company. According to another of the workers' norms, however, everyone would pitch in and work extra hard or long without extra compensation in times of emergency. The two conditions balanced out for the company, and management agreed and accepted the work crews' norms. The point is that if a change program opposes group norms, resistance is predictable. Anyone planning change would be well advised to study the norms of the groups involved by observing group action or asking group members why certain behaviors or conditions exist.

## The Involvement Dimension

The essence of the involvement principle is that people work most productively when they are involved in establishing their own goals and procedures. In such cases, they have a sense of commitment not present when goals are imposed on them.

The late Kurt Lewin found that when a group as a whole made the decision to change their method of operation, the changes were from two to ten times more effective than when group members were subjected to lectures exhorting them to change. In industry, when groups are given the responsibility for their own goals and procedures, the increase in productivity and morale is striking.

Group decision-making sometimes creates an interesting dilemma. On the one hand, some people like to participate in planning their own actions. On the other hand, when they are unaccustomed to this, conflict with people who have slightly different goals, or cannot agree on procedures, they often find it easier to rely on an authority who will tell them what to do and how to do it. Because effective involvement sometimes requires skills that group members have not developed, training in group processes may be a useful prerequisite to using the group as a vehicle for change.

When people are not involved, they can belong to a group for years and never really participate. An essential skill for leaders in tapping group forces is the ability to encourage general participation.

## The Leader-Authority Dimension

Almost all formal groups and many informal ones have a recognized leader who represents a higher status, superior position, or greater power.

It is important to observe how these leaders function in the group and how group members relate to them.

A group leader's behavior has been shown to influence the behavior of "aggressive" members. Research indicates that when children who were aggressive in a group with an authoritarian leader were shifted to a group with a democratic leadership style, their degree of aggressiveness decreased markedly. Aggression should not be considered merely a personality trait; the whole personality must be seen in the context of a particular type of group structure and climate. In another study, teenagers who were able to work effectively under either a democratic or authoritarian leader were unable to function under a laissez-faire leader who essentially let people have whatever they wanted. Too little structure led to chaos.

One study demonstrated that the leadership pattern set by the teacher affected the behavior of the students. If the teacher dominated the students, the students showed more compliance with, as well as rejection of, the teacher's domination. Moreover, the dominated students were easily distracted from schoolwork, presumably because they spent more time worrying about the teacher than about accomplishing their work. In cases where the teacher was helpful and tried to integrate the students into class activities, there was more spontaneity, initiative, cooperation between students, and effective problem-solving.

Along the same lines, another study showed that better classroom attitudes exist when students have greater opportunity to express their ideas and feelings. Their teachers would often ask questions about the students' feelings and would praise, encourage, and accept the students' feelings in a nonthreatening way. In contrast, students in classrooms with a less positive atmosphere reported that the teacher spent most of the time lecturing and giving directions and criticism. These studies all emphasize the importance of the leadership figure in the behavior of group members.

As discussed earlier, people relate to an authority figure in one of three ways: Either they are very dependent, hostile or counterdependent, or interdependent, which means they can work with the leader in a cooperative way. Some leaders encourage dependence; others are so task-oriented they do not notice the counterreactions that drain off the energies, creativity, and emotional well-being of group members. Those in leadership positions should focus on people and their needs and try to create conditions in which they can work *with* rather than *over* subordinates. To utilize the group process, one must observe the leadership-followership pattern. Who are the dominant persons or subgroups? How do group members deal with power and authority? Likert (1961) noted four predominant leadership styles in organizations—the authoritarian, the benevolent autocrat, the consultative leader, and the participative leader. Contingency theory or situationism (which emphasizes the importance of the situation) suggests that the effective leader, whatever his or her preferred style, is able to size up a situation and adopt a style consistent with situational demands. Thus, when participation is required, the leader should be able to share power with others in a collaborative process. In some groups, the leader must become more effectively participative. In other groups, the leader must become more effective in using power directly.

## The Climate or Dimension

Emotional climate or atmosphere is both real and difficult to measure. People are affected dramatically by the emotional milieu within which they live; i.e., the supportive or accepting climate in contrast to the defensive or rejecting climate. Most people have been in situations in which the prevailing mood of the group could be described as cold or formal or fun or reflective or sad. In some groups where everything seems to go right, the feeling is so good that one hates to see the meeting or activity end.

Certain ingredients create the type of climate that produces healthy interactions: adequate and helpful group standards, involvement of the total group in the problem at hand, and leaders who work *with*, not *over*, group members. Following are some other factors to consider.

### Accepting People Different from Ourselves

We are not all cut from the same cloth, and we must learn to accept others for what they have to contribute. Acceptance does not mean we must like everyone on a personal basis; we can learn to appreciate people who are quite different from ourselves. In one study, a group of managers was first asked, "Whom do you like best in the organization?" They listed their choices. Then they were asked, "Who has the best ideas in the organization?" As you might suspect, they listed the same choices. Most of us know that those we like are not uniformly brilliant, creative, sensitive, and so on. But how often do we let lack of affection distort our perceptions of people's worth?

### Showing Real, Not Pretended, Interest

Some interesting studies have indicated that we can readily detect people who are sincerely interested in others in contrast to those who only pretend an interest. Most of us have shuddered at the hearty "Well, how are we today?" issued by doctors, salesmen, and others who assume a superficial professional interest. In one study of a hospital ward, patients were asked with whom they discussed their problems. The professional staff was greatly surprised when the patients named the janitor, the elevator boy, their relatives, and the patient in the next bed. In seventy-five interviews, there was not a single mention of a doctor, a nurse, or any of the professionals working with the patients.

People can tell if others really accept them and are interested in them. There is evidence that people can *learn* to be more accepting of others. Because genuine concern is an important factor in influencing others, change agents should develop and exhibit it. They also may need to help others improve in this area.

## Giving Honest Approval and Disapproval

People like to work and live in situations in which they gain approval for work well done and are told honestly and fairly when work is below par. Too often we incorrectly assume that people to whom we are close— family, friends, colleagues—know that we approve of and like them. There is evidence that many college students are not sure that their parents love them.

In giving praise and criticism, we must beware of the so-called sandwich technique: slipping a piece of criticism between two slices of praise; i.e., "John, you did a fine job last week, *but* I want to talk to you about what you did yesterday." This practice tends to minimize the impact of the praise. Every time employees hear praise, they stiffen for the blow they know will come. Many managers could improve conditions in their organizations if they could more consistently demonstrate honest concern and approval. A change goal for some groups might be to expand the support and approval responses shared by the leader and all group members.

## Listening Instead of Always Telling

We are all aware that communication is part telling and part listening, but often our listening skills are minimal. Research indicates that regular management interviews in which managers and subordinates talk and listen to each other improve the climate. Boss (1983) has shown that effective management interviews conducted regularly following a team-building start-up prevent the regression in team-building that often occurs. He found that without follow-up, the enthusiasm generated during the first part of the team building program was lost. In contrast, boss-subordinate interviews kept the desire for action high. But the interviews must be well-planned and skillfully handled.

## Allowing People to Make Mistakes

In a defensive climate, people usually spend their time trying to defend themselves against authority figures. They do not have the time or emotional energy to be creative—to grow and mature—because their energies are dissipated in trying to protect themselves from the punishing, censoring, controlling efforts of their managers. To the degree that we can create an accepting group atmosphere, we will be increasing people's emotional health and maturity and freeing their resources for more effective collaborative work.

## The Decision-Making Dimension

When a group of people works together well, decision-making improves. Research evidence repeatedly shows that for certain kinds of problem-solving—particularly those in which every group member has some contribution to make—consensus decisions consistently will be better and more accurate, and will command a greater commitment from members than decisions made by individuals or by voting or averaging the group contributions. But it is important that the group use a consensus process through which all group members have an opportunity to express their ideas and opinions and all input is taken into account before the final decision is reached.

If the group is not working well together, the formal decision-making process may be strongly influenced by one dominant person or by a clique or subgroup. Under such conditions, decisions may not represent the best thinking of which the group is capable, nor will the group be strongly committed to implementing the decision. There are times when decisions should not be made by the total group because the problem is not amenable to group problem solving or because other constraints make an individual decision more appropriate (Timm, 1982). Part of the assessment of group process is to determine if the group is using its resources on appropriate decisions.

Sometimes people are somewhat intimidated by other group members and become quiet, nonparticipative, and unimaginative. However, if group members can learn such processes as brainstorming and sharing analogies or new ideas, the group can be a stimulus to creative thinking.

Decisions in groups are made at formal and informal levels. It is useless to make a formal decision with which group members informally disagree. Whether there will be an open discussion of the formal decision to avoid contrary informal decisions depends on certain other group dimensions already discussed, especially the influence of the authority figure and the prevailing climate.

## Two Levels of Group Activity

One of the most significant research findings has been the recognition of two levels of group action. Most groups convene for a particular task or problem-solving purpose, such as establishing a new policy or program. But we have discovered that people, like machines, cannot work indefinitely on a task without some maintenance. Too often, when people become tired, angry, frustrated, apathetic, or tense, they try to ignore these feelings and quickly complete the task before the group blows up.

The assumption is that obtaining agreement on the action to be taken is all that is needed. But if the emotional level has been neglected and people do not feel happy about the group and its work, they are ineffective in carrying out their assignments, they stay away from meetings, and they are tremendously relieved when the group finally disbands.

It is *not* a waste of time for groups to take time to clear up misunderstandings, to relieve tension, visit and relax, tell jokes, and exchange personal experiences. These are some of the maintenance functions that keep the group in a state of health so it can accomplish its task. We live in a task-oriented society in which the emphasis is on more and more production, but we neglect people's emotions at our own peril.


## Team-Building: A Method for Improving Groups

Using the dimensions described above, the overall goal of team-building is to develop a highly effective, people-building, potential releasing, goal-achieving social system. Elements characteristic of that kind of system include:

*1. Climate of high social support.* Likert (1961) describes social support this way:

> The leadership and other processes of the organization must be such as to ensure a maximum probability that in all interactions and in all relationships with the organization, each member, in the light of his background, values, desires, and expectations, will view the experience as supportive and one which builds and maintains his sense of personal worth and importance.

Others have specified a climate in which there is high trust among members, feelings of concern, fulfillment of a personal need for social interaction, and self-esteem.

*2. Open communication process.* The goal in open communication is to make all relevant data available to the decision-makers.

*3. Creative problem-solving.* As indicated earlier, the organization should be able to diagnose adequately its own problems and then formulate creative solutions to these problems.

*4. Commitment.* Following the making of decisions, the group's commitment to support and implement the decisions is essential.

*5. Achievement of individual and organizational goals.* The system must achieve that neat balance between helping individuals meet personal needs and at the same time reaching organizational goals. Organizations must be goal-oriented—that is the reason for their existence. Although personnel in the organization must help achieve the goals, a great deal of current research indicates that people are not willing to sacrifice themselves on the altar of the organization.

*6. Interdependence and team effort.* In an effective unit there is a meshing of resources as people combine their efforts to achieve goals. Interdependence is a state in which each person functions at a high level of utilization of his or her own resources as he or she uses the resources of others. The opposite of interdependence is dependency or counterdependency. In a dependency situation, the authority figure dominates and others respond passively to demands. Counterdependency represents resistant or rebellious reactions against authority. Independence connotes a condition of separateness in which people go their own ways rather than working in connection with one another.

Team effort is the result of high interdependency. This does not mean "management by committee" in the sense that no one is responsible. On a good team, each player has his or her assignment and feels responsible for its achievement but tries to combine his or her efforts with the efforts of others. The result is a synergistic effect, with the whole greater than the sum of its independent parts.

## A Team-Development Program

When signals indicate that a work unit is not functioning effectively (work is late, assignments are missed, conflicts are apparent, people are not supporting one another), it is time for the manager to consider conducting a team-building session. One must periodically stop a machine so that it gets appropriate overhaul and maintenance. So it is with human machinery, particularly a human group.

Team-development programs have been conducted with a variety of designs and formats. A simple, useful way to conduct a team-building program is the following:

1. Take at least one day off the for team-building effort and get away from the work site so there will be no interruptions.
2. Ask each person to write his or her answers to the following questions and be prepared to share them with others at the meeting:
   a) What keeps you from being as effective as you would like to be in your position?
   b) What keeps the staff (unit or department) from functioning as an effective team?
   c) What do you like about this unit that you want to maintain?
   d) What suggestions do you have for improving the quality of our working relationships and the functioning of our department?
3. At the meeting, have each person read or present his or her responses to the above questions as someone writes them on a blackboard or flipchart. There will be four lists: 1) blocks to individual effectiveness;

2) blocks to team effectiveness; 3) things people like; and 4) suggestions for improvement.

4. Ask the group to list according to priority the problems they want to address. This forms the agenda for the meeting.

5. Permit the group to begin work on achieving the goal of the team-development session: to eliminate as many obstacles as possible. This may include changing assignments, clarifying roles, clearing up misunderstandings, sharing more information, or making other innovations. The point is to engage the team in a regular examination of its own effectiveness and the development of solutions to its own problems. If a consultant is used, his or her role is to keep the team looking at its processes as it works on its problems.

Team-building is an important program for increasing the effectiveness of work units. The establishment of a program for examining work relationships, with the goal of implementing clearer arrangements, better communications, greater coordination, and better decision-making, is a sensitive process. The manager who moves in this direction should prepare well; he or she may need an outside resource person to help with the first program. But with careful planning, commitment from unit members, and a certain willingness to risk, team-building can pay big dividends. This strategy is covered in greater detail in another volume on team-building by this author. It also has been shown that team development programs result in higher performance than that of units that have not engaged in such activities (Woodman and Sherwood, 1980).

## Implications for Managing Change

The aforementioned dimensions of group life have serious implications for individual development and productivity. The groups we belong to are major determining forces in forming our likes and dislikes, establishing our goals and our methods for achieving them, determining what prejudices and attitudes we should hold, and shaping our overall maturity and health. We must tap the resources of group dynamics if we are to achieve effective plans for change, particularly in the organizational world. Team-building is one common procedure to help a group of people become more productive in their collaborative work.

Sometimes it is useful to bring in an outside process consultant (Schein, 1969) whose role is to observe the group at work and make suggestions leading to insight and change. It is also possible for a group to call time out and focus on its own processes, evaluate its own strengths and weaknesses, and plan its own action for improvement. When a group is functioning effectively, it can mobilize its resources to help implement change in a powerful fashion. When a group is bogged down in its own process problems, it is a rather weak vehicle for achieving change.

The quality circle movement offers yet another strategy for creating groups whose function it is to give the organizational leadership recommendations for improvement. Most organizations arrange for group leaders to be trained in group process before they handle a quality circle group. The quality circle is usually a composed team, not a natural work group. Its purpose is to assess existing problem areas and then recommend needed changes.

# CHAPTER 17

# Facilitating Group Process

Because the group is the vehicle for many change programs, developing skill in working with groups is essential for anyone concerned with change. The group facilitator is crucial to human-relations training, which emphasizes group process and group problem-solving and decision-making, and is also important in discussion groups, group-centered classroom situations, and group counseling or therapy. Although some training programs eliminate the trainer or facilitator, in most others he or she represents an important element in the total learning environment. According to Schein, the success of the process consultant depends upon his or her ability to deal appropriately and effectively with human interaction and group processes.

Those involved in conducting training programs or dealing with work group processes must consider the following key questions concerning their behavior:

1. How actively should the change agent/facilitator participate in the group work unit?
2. How should one intervene in the activities of the group or unit? What are the probable consequences of various types of interventions? An intervention is any action taken in an effort to influence the activities of group members.
3. What kind of relationship should be established with the group members—should one stay aloof or become one of the group?

## Types of Interventions

### Focusing on Content

In a content-focused intervention, the change agent/facilitator actually contributes to the topic of discussion. If, for example, the group is discussing "How should an effective supervisor behave?" or "What constitutes a good year-long plan?" the facilitator might share an experience, research data, or his or her opinion.

**COMMENT:** Because the behavior of the change agent/facilitator is often seen as a model for group members to follow, a content intervention may lend legitimacy to the topic and perpetuate its discussion. But if, as is usually the case, the issue is what is happening in the group "here and now," a content intervention may prevent the group from examining its own processes. Content intervention also may further the goals of the group, providing the change agent/facilitator does not offer a contribution another member might make. The agreement reached regarding the facilitator's role is important in determining how often he or she addresses content issues. The contract may or may not call for such participation.

## Focusing on Process

The facilitator focusing on process attempts to direct attention to what is currently occurring in the group. A standard intervention is for the change agent-facilitator to ask, "Why are you doing this?" Another common intervention might be to point out a process condition, such as "Were you all aware that only two persons voiced an opinion, yet a decision was made?"

**COMMENT:** There are many ways in which a change agent/facilitator may help the group focus on its own processes. The techniques employed probably are determined by one's personal style or explicit or implicit strategy for evoking the themes he or she desires to develop. Argyris (1962) says of the process intervention that begins with "I wonder": "I would not [use this phrase] because this would be dishonest. I am really *not* wondering. I believe I know why they are doing it. And perhaps more important, I believe they feel that I know. Dishonesty does not lead to authentic relationships."

It is usually more useful to point out process events with some discussion of why the event occurred and its impact on the behavior of the group members.

## Asking for Feelings

The change agent/facilitator may want to draw data from group members regarding their feelings about certain conditions or situations that have occurred in the group. An intervention of this type would be, "Ed, how did you feel when the group rejected your idea?" This is a process intervention, for it leads to consideration of what has happened. In addition, it solicits reactions to the occurrence.

**COMMENT:** Some change agent/facilitators and many participants find the sharing of feelings the most interesting part of the learning process. For some, it is the first time they have learned how others react to their behavior. Certainly this is an important and legitimate learning goal.

However, if one concentrates only on this type of intervention, a number of other important facets of group action may be neglected.

## Giving Direction

At times the change agent/facilitator may intervene to give certain suggestions, directions, procedures, or ground rules that influence the direction the group takes. In a training setting, the facilitator may structure activity by having members write out name cards, use a tape recorder, or stop at some given time. At other times, he or she may provide observation forms or suggest that the group use a group observer, try out an exercise, role-play, or experiment with a new procedure for making decisions or reaching consensus.

COMMENT: Change agent/facilitators differ in their use of direction-giving interventions. Some offer direction only in the form of suggestions; others, by virtue of their status position, impose certain actions on group members. Both positions have a rationale: Those preferring suggestion believe that group members should make their own decisions, and those favoring imposed direction feel group members should learn to cope with directive behavior, particularly if it causes resentment.

If one has great need to control, one may intervene often or else recognize this need in oneself and overreact by withholding direction from the group when it would be helpful. A critical point is frequently reached when the group is floundering and not learning or achieving results. The change agent/facilitator must then decide whether to let the group waste time and suffer frustration while working through its own impasse or to risk reinforcing dependency by supplying direction. In such situations, he or she must consider such factors as the length of time he or she will be working with the group, the group's level of dependency, the resources available to the group, and his or her own tolerance for ambiguity.

## Giving Direct Feedback

Sometimes the change agent/facilitator may intervene by giving direct feedback to a member or to the group as a whole. When and how this is done depends on his or her strategy. It may be necessary to set the norm for giving feedback by starting the process. If one group member intimidates others, the change agent/facilitator may need to open up the situation with feedback.

COMMENT: Some facilitators prefer to give direct feedback early in their experience with the group, both as a model for group members and to legitimize this type of response. Others prefer to wait until they have worked through any authority problems with group members. Here again the change agent/facilitator faces a dilemma. Group members are often eager, and properly so, to know how the only trained person present sees the group and its individual members. The facilitator's reactions, however, may be no more valid or important than feedback from other group members. Thus, the facilitator must contribute feedback and at the same time encourage the group to appreciate feedback data from all its members.

## Providing Cognitive Models or Insights

Occasionally the facilitator may desire to discuss general theory or information elaborating, clarifying, or providing insight into an experience the group has had. Some may give a "lecturette" or talk briefly with the group.

COMMENT: The change agent/facilitator must confront the question, "If I take time to provide the insight, will it heighten the learning process, or will the participants learn more if they form the same insight from their own experiences?" He or she must be careful not to monopolize the group's time by dispensing a great deal of cognitive information, perhaps satisfying his or her own need to be seen as an expert but minimizing the benefit that comes from letting people learn for themselves.

## Performing Group Task-Maintenance Functions

There is ample evidence that a series of task and maintenance activities must be performed if a group is to accomplish its task and remain an effective human system. In work units and training groups, the change agent/facilitator often intervenes and performs a number of the task-maintenance functions necessary to promote learning or work, or helps the group realize that such functions are important.

*1. Opinion-seeking.* Group members are asked for their reactions to what has happened in the group.

*2. Opinion-giving.* Group members share opinions as to what they think is occurring in the group.

*3. Initiating.* Initiating, which is similar to direction-giving, may take the form of suggestions for a new group goal or a new definition of the problem. It may take the form of a suggested solution or a means of handling a difficulty that the group has encountered. It may take the form of a proposed procedure for the group or a new way of organizing the group for the task ahead.

*4. Elaborating.* Someone expands or develops an idea already presented by others.

*5. Coordinating.* Someone tries to pull together different ideas or suggestions already introduced into the group.

**6.** *Summarizing.* Someone summarizes what has occurred or some of the important insights gained.

**7.** *Consensus-testing.* Someone asks group members if they were in agreement concerning a certain decision or action.

**8.** *Performing Technical Procedures.* The person performing technical functions expedites group action by performing routine tasks; e.g., distributing materials, adjusting physical conditions for the group by rearranging the seating or running the recording machine, etc. This represents a physical intervention in the group.

**9.** *Reality-testing.* When the group suggests that a member behave in a certain way or try out certain actions, someone intervenes and helps members explore whether these actions are really possible or desirable.

Maintenance functions include the following:

**1.** *Encouraging.* Someone intervenes by praising, supporting, or otherwise accepting the contributions of group members.

**2.** *Harmonizing.* Someone intervenes by trying to reconcile differences between group members.

**3.** *Gate-keeping.* Someone encourages or facilitates participation by group members.

**4.** *Standard-setting.* Someone expresses a standard or norm he or she feels would help the group reach its goals.

**COMMENT:** When and how often the facilitator performs various task-maintenance functions for the group depends on his or her strategy. Some will intervene extensively early in task-maintenance functions, not only to provide a model for group participants, but also to get certain important things done. Because group members have not yet developed an understanding of these functions or the ability to perform them, the facilitator supplies them as needed. As members develop greater ability to perform these group functions, the facilitator may reduce his or her own efforts. Then, when certain functions are needed, he or she may intervene to focus on process and ask why they have not been carried out.

## Diagnosing

From time to time the change agent/facilitator may present to the group his or her diagnosis of its progress. This may be done through a hypothesis or series of hypotheses concerning the group's current status. For example, group members may recognize apathy among themselves and be at a loss to understand or explain it. The facilitator may intervene with a diagnosis such as, "There are a number of possibilities why the group is apathetic. One hypothesis is that your goals are either unclear or too broad. Another hypothesis is that you are afraid that if you resume work you may reopen old conflicts." He or she then may ask group members for other possibilities or suggest that they examine their reactions to the general apathy. This intervention is designed to provoke the group into a diagnosis of group problems.

**COMMENT:** A diagnostic intervention is somewhere between opinion-giving and development of theory or insight (cognitive orientation). It is an exploratory, suggestive, hypothesizing comment, the purpose of which is the understanding of group processes.

## Protecting Group Members

In another type of intervention, the facilitator interrupts at certain points to protect individual members. Whether this type of intervention is in one's repertoire depends on one's theory of training or consulting. Its purpose is to prevent group members from "overexposing" their behavior by sharing personal incidents, feelings, or reactions that may not be appropriate to the goals of the group. Overexposure may create a situation that neither the group nor the facilitator find productive or useful.

One may feel a need to protect a group member if feedback to that person is ill-timed or unnecessarily severe. It also may be necessary to protect the individuality of a member, to allow him or her to maintain his or her own identity despite group pressure to conform.

**COMMENT:** Some professionals would not use this intervention but would instead focus on the process and ask the group if their behavior was appropriate to the goals. A direct protection intervention would call for the facilitator to say, "Joe, I think you are going too far at this point."

## Interventions and Strategy

A change agent/facilitator's intervention is only part of the total strategy or overall plan for implementing the learning goals he or she has established. It involves such factors as:

1. *Timing:* When and how often does one intervene?
2. *Issues:* Around what concerns does one intervene?
3. *Emotion:* How much of one's own emotional makeup is funneled into the group (humor, anger, praise, warmth)?
4. *Structure:* How much control does one maintain over the group?
5. *Interpersonal Relations:* What is one's relationship with group members? Does one try to become a group member, maintain one's unique status, interact with group members outside the group?
6. *Theory of Individual and Group Behavior:* One's own orientation concerning individual and group dynamics will determine in part what one observes, on what issues one tries to focus, and what material one will emphasize.

Facilitators and consultants frequently ask, "What strategy or strategies are most effective in bringing about desired goals?" Thus far, little attempt has been made to answer this question objectively. At this point, at least, training is much more of an art than a science. Although it may never be possible or desirable to reduce training procedures to a standardized set of responses, it is nevertheless important to ascertain what style or strategy produces maximum learning.

One way to objectify training for research and analytical purposes is to systematically observe and catalog the interventions mentioned above to determine what pattern of intervention maximizes quantifiable learning goals.

## Interventions and the Facilitator as a Person

Starting with a study by Reisel (1962), it has often been observed that the facilitator's personality affects the types of interventions he or she makes. Reisel demonstrates that along with explicit or implicit strategy, other forces influence facilitators' professional behavior. They will intervene in terms of their own needs to control, to be accepted and liked, and to succeed. They exhibit their own peculiar patterns of responding to anxiety, conflict, and ambiguity. Moreover, they may not be aware of how these internal forces influence their behavior in the training or consulting process.

In addition to these deep-seated emotional dimensions, the change agent/facilitator also has language and speech patterns, physical mannerisms, and gestures that become part of the intervention. Thus, the type of intervention and its strategic application plus certain personality traits of the facilitator in combination affect the intervention.

One can hypothesize that someone with strong needs to control might use more direction-giving, cognitive orientation, direct feedback, and summarizing interventions. The change agent/facilitator who avoids conflicts and the revelation of emotions may find it more comfortable to make content and direction interventions and to perform harmonizing functions when conflict occurs.

## Implications for Managing Change

If a change attempt includes a change agent functioning as a process consultant to a work group, facilitator for a team-building program, or trainer, his or her group strategy and skills are critical for success. Strategy includes the overall goal one is trying to achieve with the group and the plan of action to achieve the goal. The skills include the ability to observe, diagnose, and take needed action in the group process so that the plan is implemented and the goal achieved. A change agent who uses the group as a vehicle for change must develop an appropriate strategy and set of skills.

# CHAPTER 18
# System Diagnosis and Change

Planning for change is a constant need in any organization. There are always conditions, results, and consequences that managers are trying to modify in one way or another. One set of conditions ripe to be changed (hereafter referred to as "direct organizational outputs") are such factors as profit/loss, production, costs, wastage, and quality. These are the direct, usually measurable consequences of the efforts of those working in the system. Remedial action soon follows whenever one of these conditions varies in an undesirable direction. A second set of consequences of deep concern to managers is the "intermediate outputs." These factors, which are often less measurable but equally important to worker morale and subsequent direct organizational outputs, include such conditions as conflict, apathy, job satisfaction, motivation, innovation, teamwork, etc. (see Table 18.1). When these conditions begin to deteriorate, managers become concerned because negative intermediate conditions eventually affect the direct output factors. Steps to reverse such trends are based on a diagnosis of the factors responsible for the drop-off in the intermediate or output variable. The adequacy of one's diagnostic ability—thinking appropriately in terms of cause and effect—significantly affects the action taken, which in turn influences output.

If the diagnosis is poor, the action designed to improve output factors probably will result in inadequate change in the direction desired. Most organization managers and change agents—whether in business, government, volunteer or service organization, or the home—already have developed some diagnostic schema. For example, poor performance may be ascribed to "laziness" or personality conflicts or hiring the wrong people or loss of the work ethic among the young.

This presentation will examine a model of three interlocking internal systems that affect outputs and also address the impact of the external environment. Table 18.1 shows that according to this model, intermediate and direct output variables result from three interlocking internal systems: the social system, the technical/operation system, and the administrative system. Although all three systems affect outputs to some degree, at a given time one system may be most significant. If such is the case, it is important to take appropriate action in the dominant influencing system

## TABLE 18.1
## Systems That Influence Organization Outputs

**External Systems**

| Customers Clients | Unions Government | Suppliers Competition | Mass Media Publics |
|---|---|---|---|

**Internal Systems**

| Social System | Technical or Operation System | Administrative System | = | Intermediate Outputs | = | Direct Organizational Outputs |
|---|---|---|---|---|---|---|
| Climate | Equipment | Policies | | Grievances | | Production |
| Decision Making | Material | Rules-Regulations | | Morale | | P/L |
| Interaction-Influence | Physical Layout | Procedures | | Apathy | | Quality |
| Leadership | Work Arrangements | Wage-Salary | | Satisfaction | | Costs |
| Communications | Work Flow | Promotions | | Conflict | | Service |
| Rewards-Punishments | Location | Budgets | | Turnover | | Sales |
| Individuals | Size-Numbers | Audits | | Commitment | | |
| | | Reports | | | | |
| | | Structure | | | | |

to achieve desired results. Moreover, an organization may be affected by external demand or client systems that must be understood and managed.

# System Diagnosis

This chapter will focus primarily on those forces that function inside the organization. All organizations are open systems in the sense that they interact with the outside environment; all organizations both influence and are influenced by that environment. The open-system framework is presented in more detail in a later chapter.

# Three Internal Organizational Systems

## The Social System

Every organization has its social world, a dynamic atmosphere composed of people in different positions interacting—talking, arguing, helping, deciding, solving problems—to achieve the goals of the organization and to satisfy their own personal needs. Every social system has the following basic components:

   *1. Climate.* The prevailing emotional state shared by members of the system, the climate may be formal, relaxed, defensive, cautious, accepting, or trusting.

   *2. Communication Network.* There are formal and informal patterns governing who talks with whom, when, how often, and about what. Some people are excluded from the network; some networks share more data than do others.

   *3. Status-Role Relationships.* Organizations require some division of labor, whereby workers perform various functions assume various roles. Because certain functions are more highly regarded, some people have higher status than others, and therefore more power and usually more influence.

   *4. Style of Management/Supervision or Leadership.* Some workers in the organization are placed in superordinate positions relative to others, and have subordinates of their own. The prevalent pattern or style of managing superordinates usually starts at the top.

   *5. Decision-Making Method.* A basic process in any organization is to solve problems and make decisions. Thus, a method for handling problem-solving and decision-making requirements becomes established in the social system. It is closely linked to the pattern of management but also addresses whether decisions are made by few or many, the use of relevant resources in problem-solving, the creativity applied to decisions, and the degree of commitment to implementing decisions.

**6.** *Values and Goals.* Organizations differ in the values its members hold. One organization may value service to customers, while another values creativity among employees. Some of these values become ends toward which effort is expended; they become the goals of the system. Social systems differ in terms of their goals, how values and goals are established, and the degree to which members accept the values and goals and work toward them. In the same organization, one unit could value group participation while another would value high-quality individual effort.

**7.** *Individuals.* Social systems vary in many of their processes depending on the kinds of people who compose the system. For example, one expects a group of older workers to behave differently than a group in its early adult years. Only recently has the mix of individuals—minority groups, women, age levels, etc.—become a major organizational concern. Now it is an important consideration both legally and strategically.

## The Technical System

Every organization develops a method—the unique arrangement of equipment, material, people, processes—used to accomplish work. A common industrial technical system is the assembly line, in which workers are arranged along a conveyor belt. As the product to be assembled moves along the belt, each worker does a specific task. The system can be altered by changing equipment, using different basic or raw materials, arranging people differently, or changing work assignments.

It is immediately apparent that the social system is integrally connected with the technical system: The physical placement of people affects their ability to communicate with one another. Work assignments and work flow influence the pattern of management used and perhaps the ways decisions are made. This interplay between the social system and the technical aspects of work is commonly referred to as the sociotechnical system.

However, there are elements unique to the technical system, as distinct from the social system, that can be altered separately (although concomitant effects in the social system may be noticed. For example, in a common university technical system, a professor stands at a podium in the front of a large lecture hall speaking for a whole period. If the class were broken up into small groups of students arranged in a circle around the professor, a different learning process would probably occur. But if the professor were afflicted with notions of status and his or her superior role, he or she might continue to dominate the situations, to lecture, and to control the social system. For real change to take place, modification is necessary in both the technical and social systems, so the professor at the podium would probably find it almost impossible to change the basic nature of instruction unless changes were made in the existing technical system.

## The Administrative System

Interlacing the social and technical systems is a network of policy, procedure, auditing, reporting, and formal structure that represents another whole system functioning in connection with the other two but remaining somewhat separate. Every organization has established certain formalized procedures for setting down standards, rules, and regulations that influence the other two systems. Important elements in this administrative system are as follows:

*1. Wage and Salary Administration.* Organizations establish procedures to set pay levels and regulate increases in salary, bonuses, and benefits.

*2. Hiring, Firing, and Promotions.* The administrative system of each organization develops methods for hiring, firing and making promotions.

*3. Report-Auditing.* Many organizations collect data in the form of report-making or auditing on such matters as use of materials, finances, work output, and quality control.

*4. Fringe Benefits.* More and more, organizations are establishing criteria and methods for allocating fringe benefits such as vacations, sick leave, retirement funds, and insurance.

*5. Budgets.* The building of the budget is a critical issue in determining the priorities and activities of every unit in an organization.

*6. Organization Structure.* This represents the hierarchical arrangements of units and functions—who is connected with whom in reporting and working relationships.

# Organization Change by System Intervention

Research on organizations provides numerous examples of change attempts (some successful and some not) based on the alteration of some aspect of one or more of the three systems.

## The Administrative System

One of the simplest and most common ways to implement organizational change occurs in the administrative system. The old Hawthorne studies described such attempts to improve production in a work setting (Roethlisberger and Dickson, 1939). When workers in the bank wiring room were offered a bonus if they exceeded the existing level of production, production remained constant. Data collected from the workers revealed that through the informal social system, the workers thought that if they increased production to get the bonus, management would either raise the base production level or lay people off because fewer workers could maintain the previous level. Because the existing situation was satisfactory to the workers, they decided to continue producing at the existing level.

And because they agreed that lower production brought tighter supervision, they did not permit production to drop. They applied informal sanctions to one another when informal norms were violated. Thus, an attempt to alter production by offering a bonus—a change in the administrative system—was not successful because of contrary conditions in the social system.

A management consultant recalls a situation in which the management of a production division became disturbed over obscene words written on the walls of the workers' restroom. Concerned that the graffiti reflected poorly on the company, management issued a memo to the workers to the effect that this practice must stop immediately. Sending new orders via memo is a common administrative method for trying to induce change. Evidently the workers interpreted the message as a challenge; obscenities increased and continued even after threats of punishment. A series of strategy-counterstrategy moves ensued, including a monitor stationed in the restrooms. Reduced to repainting the walls every day at considerable expense, management finally decided that some obscene words were not worth all that trouble. The measures were stopped, and the number of obscenities dropped to the few there had been in the first place.

Most parents have tried the strategy of manipulating the administrative system as a means of inducing better performance in children. To encourage children to study more, practice a musical instrument, clean up their rooms, or do their chores, parents often offer greater rewards such as larger allowances or more television, or invoke penalties such as no television or no allowance or no use of the car. This domestic manipulation of the reward-punishment aspect of the administrative system reportedly has limited positive effects.

The research literature on organizations is replete with examples of experiments in altering the administrative system to influence organization outputs. Results have varied. Manipulating wage and salary conditions is a common strategy (Rothe, 1960). One study showed that when needle-threaders in an English factory were put on a piece-rate system in order to reward those who worked harder, individual production dropped from ninety-six dozen needles a day to seventy-five dozen a day. However, when workers were told they could go home when they reached a quota of 100 dozen per day, production immediately jumped. On the average, workers reached their quota two-and-a-half hours early each day. Apparently, *money* incentives were not as important as *time* incentives to these women; consequently, an administrative change in wages was not as important as the time factor.

Apparently, some improvements in organization outputs can be achieved by changing certain administrative practices, such as decreasing labor turnover through better methods of personnel selection (Fleishman and Berniger, 1960).

Regarding the reduction of accidents on the job, though, a study in a large tractor factory demonstrated that the factor most highly correlated with accidents was the degree of comfort in the shop environment. Men working in physically uncomfortable environments were most likely to be injured. In this case, attempts to reduce accidents through signs, awards, and threats apparently were not as effective as a change in the technical system (Keenan, Kerr, and Sherman, 1951).

## The Social System

Ross and Zander (1959) compared employees in the same company who terminated their work situation with those who stayed and found a major difference in the degree to which certain psychological needs were met. They state:

> In this study we establish the fact that the degree of satisfaction of certain personal needs supplied by a person's place of employment has a significant direct relationship to his continuing to work for that company. These personal needs are for recognition, for autonomy, for a feeling of doing work that is important, and for evaluation by fair standards. In addition, knowing important people in the organization is related to continued employment.

The fulfillment of these needs is a direct consequence of events within the social system. Employees are recognized, evaluated, and given a feeling of doing worthwhile work in a context of working with others in the organization. Changes in the operation system might affect autonomy, but changes in the administrative system without modification in the social system appear to have minimal effect. A great deal has been written about the effects of the pattern of management or supervision on organization outputs. This has been a major variable in research. Supervision is related to productivity, but the degree of influence, though important, is surprisingly low. Argyle and his associates conclude: "The differences in productivity in work groups resulting from contrasting methods of supervision were typically small, usually not larger than 15 percent of the total output" (Argyle, Gardner, and Ciofi, 1958). The management pattern also is related to grievances and turnover (Fleishman and Harris, 1962).

Dubin (1965), in summarizing the research on supervision and productivity, has this to say:

> There is no "one best" method of supervision. As in all human systems, there is variability in the systems of supervision of industrial and commercial work. Several styles of supervision are effective, but they are individually successful only in relation to appropriate work settings. Variety in supervisory behaviors may no longer be considered a challenge to choose the "one best" for all settings, but rather as a challenge to understand where each does or does not work. (p. 47)

Dubin's analysis indicates that the type of supervision is related to the type of operation system; differing operation systems, such as unit production, mass production, and continuous production, require alterations in management behavior.

In an extensive case analysis, Guest shows the effects on a manufacturing plant of a new plant manager with a different style of management. The new manager introduced a number of changes in the social system, including regular report meetings at which communications were opened to all supervisors in the plant. In addition, he altered the operation system by improving physical comfort in the working areas, relocating ovens in the paint department, changing the number and length of conveyor lines in the trim department, and replacing outmoded tools. As a result of these changes in both the social and operation systems (with supporting administrative changes), the output variables also changed remarkably. Labor costs were reduced 14 percent; manufacturing costs, previously highest in the industry, dropped to 15 percent lower than those of the next best performer; absenteeism dropped from 4.1 percent to 2.5 percent; and turnover dropped from 6.1 percent to 4.9 percent. In comparison to other plants, this one became a leader in quality, safety, indirect labor costs, and lack of grievances (Guest, 1962).

Another case study, by Marrow, Bowers, and Seashore (1967), describes the changes in output variables as a result of major changes in management patterns in the textile industry. In this case, a company was acquired. After changes were introduced, especially in the social system, the performance of operators improved. Changes in the technical and administrative systems also were made. The authors conclude that the following changes were most important to the productivity of operators:

1. An earnings development program through which individual operators received individual counseling and help.
2. The weeding out of low earners.
3. Training in interpersonal relations for supervisors and staff.
4. Consultation and problem-solving with groups of operators.

These authors state: "Although the technical changes . . . were on a large scale and affected nearly every employee, we find from our analysis that these changes cannot be shown to have improved operator performance."

It appears that items 1, 3, and 4 are changes in the social system, and item 2—the weeding out of low earners—is a change in the administrative system: that is, a change in policy regarding low earners.

Likert (1967), in a study of management in the sales division of a large organization, found that managers of all top sales units had a high supportive style of management, high performance goals, and a well-organized sales plan. Managers in the low-producing sales units had low scores in supportive relations and performance goals, both of which Likert regards as essential:

> The preceding analysis shows that a manager who has high performance goals and excellent job organization but who relies solely on economic needs and direct pressure to motivate his men is very likely to be disappointed by their achievements. The noneconomic motives must be used fully, along with the economic needs, to create high performance goals and establish the level of motivational forces which yield high productivity. (p. 64)

## The Technical/Operational System

Frederick Herzberg, one of the strong exponents of the importance of the operation system in contributing to output variables, considers social and administrative system variables as essentially *hygiene* factors—factors that remove hazards from the environment but are not true motivators toward greater achievement. For him, the motivators lie in the nature of the job itself, and any basic change in motivation and hence ouput must stem from change in the nature of the technical system. He says:

> Supervisory training in human relations is probably essential to the maintenance of good hygiene at work. This is particularly true for the many jobs, both at rank and file and managerial levels, in which modern industry offers little chance for the operation of the motivators. These jobs are atomized, cut and dried, monotonous. They offer little chance for responsibility and achievement and thus little opportunity for self-actualization. . . . A man who finds his job challenging, exciting, and satisfying will perhaps tolerate a difficult supervisor. (Herzberg, Mausner, and Snyderman, 1959, p. 45)

Herzberg (1968) describes the marked change in output variables (increased productivity, lower turnover, and absenteeism) in a work situation in which employees doing routine correspondence were allowed to enlarge the nature of their work and assume more responsibility for their own output. Such modifications, which lead to increased responsibility, challenge, and opportunity for growth, are the real motivators, according to Herzberg.

McGregor (1967), who also recognized the importance of the operation system as it affects organization outputs, discussed three different studies showing how operational changes affect outputs. In a coal mine in Britain, a textile mill in India, and an electronics firm in America, the basic operation system was changed from one in which the individual worker does a small specialized piece of the work to one in which each worker functions on a team producing the whole product. In each case, productivity increased up to 30 percent.

There is a difference between making a change in the basic work flow and changing the physical conditions of the basic work operation. The Hawthorne studies began with an experiment pertaining to the effects of illumination on productivity. As expected, as lighting improved, production increased. However, much to the surprise of the researchers, as lighting decreased, production reached an all-time high. It became apparent that the workers' social system mandated that they should work harder because they were participating in an experiment. Here, it was the motivation created by the social system rather than the lighting that affected output.

Later in the Hawthorne experiments, modifications were made in the operation system of a relay assembly test room through the introduction of rest periods. Output increased markedly. But when rest periods were eliminated, production reached an all-time high. An analysis of this situation indicated that production was more a function of a close-knit social system than of the alteration of work with rest periods (Roethlisberger and Dickson, 1939).

Baveles and Strauss (Whyte, 1955) describe a situation in a toy factory where employees working in the paint section of an assembly line complained of poor air circulation and demanded fans. Although engineers maintained that fans would not help, production increased slightly after fans were provided. Next, the employees requested the right to regulate the speed of the assembly-line conveyor belt to correspond with their physical condition—faster when they felt fresh and slower when they were tired. This was permitted, and production improved sharply. Not surprisingly, the increased production from this section of the assembly line resulted in pressures on workers on either side of the paint crew. When the other workers complained bitterly, the management eliminated the modifications in the paint section and the foreman and many of the workers in the paint crew promptly resigned. This example underlines the necessity of seeing the interlocking nature of a total operational system and of awareness that change in one part may affect other parts.

Whyte's classic study of the restaurant industry determined that in certain restaurants, the operation system was based on tasks performed by the waitress who took the customer's order and passed the order directly to the cook, thus initiating work for him. Cooks often responded negatively to a lower-status waitress initiating their work and would frustrate the waitress by delaying the orders. When the work flow was altered by eliminating contact between waitress and cook by placing a spindle or barrier between them and when orders were passed in written form, tensions and disturbances decreased (Whyte, 1948).

Perhaps tension and conflicts between waitresses and cooks could be reduced at the social system level through human relations training and mutual acceptance and cooperation. However, alteration of the technical operation system appears to be more easily accomplished.

## TABLE 18.2
## System Conditions That Seem to Affect Output Variables

| Social System | Technical/ Operation System | Administrative System |
|---|---|---|
| • Workers are involved in setting goals and making decisions. | • Physical conditions are comfortable and safety conditions prevail. | • Rules and regulations are jointly established by management and workers when feasible. |
| • Communications are open; people are kept informed about events in the system. | • Operation system allows workers to interact and build social support. | • Policies and procedures do not restrict adequate development of the social system. |
| • High level of trust and acceptance exists. | • Workers are responsible for the quality of output of the operation system. | • Formal rewards are given for appropriate management and worker behavior. |
| • Management is highly person-centered as well as concerned about production. | • Workers have some control over the operation system; they are not entirely controlled by it. | • Benefits are distributed in an equitable fashion. |
| • Management has high performance goals. | • Operation system requirements are matched to an adequate degree to the personal resources of the workers. | • Procedures and rules are flexible and amenable to modification. |
| • Workers feel needed, useful, engaged in something worthwhile. | • Workers have an opportunity to use a variety of skills and abilities on the job. | • Workers are involved in setting goals and planning work. |
| • Team spirit develops; workers have pride in their work group. | • Operation system does not require too many conflicting interfaces. | • Restrictive reporting and auditing as control measures are not used. |
| • Workers feel support, recognition from supervisors and others. | | • Authority and responsibility are appropriately delegated. |

| Social System | Technical/ Operation System | Administrative System |
|---|---|---|
| *continued* | | |
| • Workers receive "coaching" or help when needed. | | • Advancements and promotions result from open review between superior and subordinate. |
| • No undue pressure is exerted. | | |

Passmore (1982) has considered the blocks to restructuring work that emerge in any of the three systems. Advance recognition of potential blocks can be helpful in expediting a restructuring program.

## Principle of System Reinforcement

An examination of the above framework and the supporting research evidence leads to the development of the following working principle: To maximize ouput variables, all three systems (social, operation, and administrative) should function in such a way that they are mutually reinforcing. Table 18.2 identifies the conditions necessary in the three systems to support desired organization outputs.

It is essential that a social system foster pride in the work group, mutual support interdependence between management and worker, and high trust and acceptance. Such a social system is hampered by a technical operation system that keeps people isolated, working independently with no chance for interaction, and whose quality controls were not developed by the workers. A desirable social system also is inhibited by an administrative system that requires close supervision, a tight audit and reporting procedure, secret reviews of performance, unilateral allocation of rewards, tight control of expenditures, and delegation of authority only to assign work.

Similarly, it is extremely difficult to establish a creative operation system or to revamp the administrative system if the social system does not function well. If the social system management is oppressive and controlling, decisions are not shared, communications are closed, trust is low, and people are highly dependent or rebellious, then the possibility of new, creative procedures and work systems will be drastically reduced.

Those trying to influence output variables often are unaware of the interconnections in the systems. For example, a growing company implementing a new policy of decentralization delegated more authority and autonomy to plants in separate locations. Along with their increased responsibility, however, managers were not given control over capital expenditures; they were obliged to clear all expenditures over a few hundred dollars with the executive committee. Under this policy, it was difficult to achieve the goals of decentralization.

Automation, which represents a major alteration of the operation system, is an increasing trend in industry. Such a drastic modification of operations of necessity requires appropriate changes in the social and administrative systems. Some analysis of these trends already has been undertaken.

## Implications for Managing Change

It has been proposed that organization outputs are a function of the effects of three interlocking internal systems—social, operation, and administrative—as well as influences from the external environment. Alteration of outputs requires modification of all three internal systems, at least insofar as a modification in one system should be supported by appropriate alterations in the others. Much of the current writing about organization development focuses primarily on changes in the social system. However, total organization development demands sound diagnosis of all systems that affect output and appropriate decisions for change based on that diagnosis.

When intermediate or direct output factors are not satisfactory, it is mandatory that the causal factors be uncovered. Good data collection and analysis are vital in making an appropriate diagnosis and developing a plan of action. The issue of possible actions or interventions has been discussed at length elsewhere (Dyer, 1983). It is critical that "root" causal factors be addressed in the change plan. If the basic problem is located in the technical system, a change in the administrative system only is almost a guarantee of failure.

# CHAPTER 19

# Open-System Analysis and Planning

Most current research and theory concerning organizations is based on a closed-system model. For purposes of analysis, the organization is presumed to be contained within the confines of its physical operating structures and the existing organization chart. According to the closed-system model, an automobile assembly plant, for example, is seen as a set of workers, in a particular location, producing cars. If output is reduced or restructed, diagnosis and change action generally take place within the confines of the plant.

Almost all organization theorists, however, recognize that any organization exists within a wider environment and can be influenced considerably by conditions outside its walls. The automobile plant is affected by general economic conditions, government regulations on automotive safety and pollution-reducing equipment, demands of labor unions, availability and cost of raw materials, taxes, prices of competing products, and on and on. In this sense the organization is an "open system." Planning must accommodate the external environment, the components of which appear in Figure 19.1.

The outside environment supplies inputs that are processed or converted by the organization, via its work, or throughout activities, into outputs. Outputs go back into the environment and may subsequently alter or influence new inputs, which again are funneled into the system. This is an ongoing cycle for all organizations.

The automobile plant takes in from the environment its supply of labor, raw materials, and equipment. In addition, if management is wise, it takes in all possible information regarding such external conditions as prices, markets, taxes, regulations, and the like. This data is considered in formulating decisions on wages, pricing, dividends paid to investors, public relations activities, markets, and expansion or reduction possibilities. The internal or "closed" part of the organization processes the inputs through its production setup—assembly line, groups of craftspeople, or service departments—and transforms the inputs into a product or service that is once again returned to the outside environment.

A similar procedure recurs daily: Workers entering the company from the outside environment bring with them attitudes, reactions, and feelings

**Figure 19.1** External Environment Organization

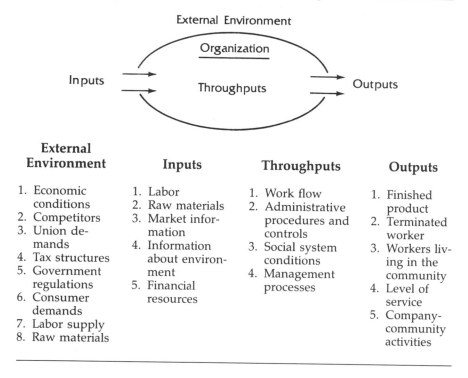

| External Environment | Inputs | Throughputs | Outputs |
|---|---|---|---|
| 1. Economic conditions<br>2. Competitors<br>3. Union demands<br>4. Tax structures<br>5. Government regulations<br>6. Consumer demands<br>7. Labor supply<br>8. Raw materials | 1. Labor<br>2. Raw materials<br>3. Market information<br>4. Information about environment<br>5. Financial resources | 1. Work flow<br>2. Administrative procedures and controls<br>3. Social system conditions<br>4. Management processes | 1. Finished product<br>2. Terminated worker<br>3. Workers living in the community<br>4. Level of service<br>5. Company-community activities |

that may influence their work during the throughput activity. At the end of the day, they return to the community environment and discharge their feelings and reactions about the company. If their feelings are positive, the community believes the company is good; people want to work for the company and use its products or services. Thus, the resource loop is completed: What goes out eventually influences what comes in. Pickhardt (1981) has noted that problems occur in an organization when new members bought in from the outside must be connected with the existing work group. By rejecting the input (new members), the old group demonstrates the difficulty of changing input without preparing the system.

## The Wider Environment Inside an Organization

The above model considers the whole organization as its exists in the total community or societal environment. In a similar sense, members of each department or subunit of a large organization could regard the total organization as their wider environment and consequently concentrate on interacting more effectively with other departments.

For example, a purchasing department is influenced by the policies, procedures, budgets, and constraints of other departments. Purchasing takes in as inputs requests for service from other departments, processes those requests, and generates completed transactions as outputs. If the outputs are satisfactory, the wider environment (other departments and management) will provide more inputs in the form of increased requests for service. On the other hand, if the outputs are poor in quality, inputs decrease, and the usefulness of the purchasing department is diminished.

# Improving Effectiveness with the Outside Environment

*Open-system planning* is the term used to describe the process by which an organization or subunit of an organization plans to improve its interactions with those parts of its wider environment essential to its well-being. Following are some important elements in effective open-system planning:

## 1. Identification and Specification of the "Core Mission"

Every organization or unit must define for itself and its members its basic goal, function, or "reason for being." It is difficult to relate to environmental demands unless the "core mission" or purpose of the organization is clearly understood. Sometimes organizations are distracted by concerns not directly related to their core mission. For example, although a university defines its purpose as training undergraduates to cope effectively with modern society, university administrators may find that they spend too much time and effort seeking and supporting research projects that are tangential to their mission. It is also possible that an organization's core mission is composed of several parts, some more important than others.

## 2. Identification of Important Clients or Demand Systems

Having determined their organization's core mission, those planning to deal with the outside environment must identify important external clients (those using their products or services) and demand systems (those who make demands of some kind on the organization).

For the automobile plant, important clients may be all former buyers of their product and a critical demand system may be the automobile workers' labor union. Both these components of the wider environment must be considered in formulating plans and programs.

## 3. "Is" and "Ought" Planning

Planners must write out clear and detailed descriptions of "how it is" with each particular client and demand system. How are the relationships, the interactions, the amount of contact with each external unit? What about its responsiveness and reactions? It may be necessary to gather current data from the client or demand systems in order to grasp the situation accurately.

After describing "how it is," the planner must assess whether the current situation is desirable. If not, the planner must state how things "ought to be" if the relationship were at an optimum level. If a manager cannot determine the current relationship with a particular client or demand unit, he or she must spend time gathering data from the external systems.

### 4. Current Response to Clients and Demands

Having described how things are and how they ought to be, organization planners now must delineate the current level of response to the client and, using accurate data as a base, answer these questions: What does this client want from us? What are we currently doing for this client? Is our current response to the client or the demand moving us closer to where we would like to be?

### 5. Action Planning

Having determined how things ought to be and whether or not the current response is adequate, planners must decide what actions to take to achieve the desired state of affairs. The plan should include answers to these questions:

1. What actions must be taken to move in the desired direction?
2. Who should be taking this action?
3. What resource costs and allocations are necessary?
4. What is the timetable for action? When should action start and finish?
5. How will we ensure follow-through? Who will report on progress? When will a progress report be due?
6. How will we evaluate or measure the action to be sure of achieving our objectives?

## Open System Mapping

Mapping is another method for planning change in connection with the demands of the external environment. This involves drawing a map and using circles to indicate the various individuals and organizations that comprise the environment and their relationship to one another (see Figure 19.2). A second map can be drawn to represent how one wants the environment to be. The planning process addresses how to move from the status quo to the ideal circumstances.

————— **Figure 19.2**   Open System Map of Television Station RVP —————

(a) map as the station is

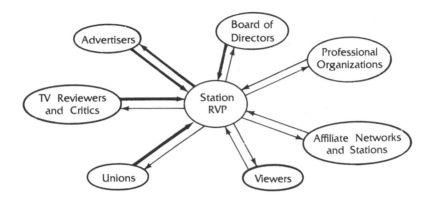

(b) map of station as one would like it to be

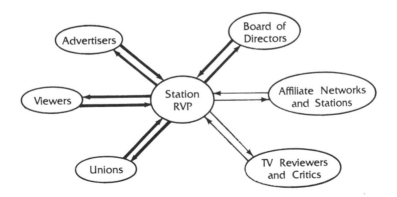

Changes from what is, to what one would like it to be, include: (1) raise the importance of viewers and amount of reciprocal communication; (2) equalize communications between station and board, advertisers, critics, and unions.

# Implications for Managing Change

Only recently have managers and change agents begun to develop systematic plans for influencing the external environment. Open-system planning and mapping are methods employed to change the responses and reactions of people or units outside the organization who use or influence the organization's outputs. Much current literature on management pertains only to management of people and conditions *inside* the organization. Inside management always will be important, but no organization is secure without a program for assessing and improving relationships with outside demands.

# CHAPTER 20

# Organizational Culture: Analysis and Change*

In an earlier chapter, an analysis was presented of the organization as a complex system made up of interlocking subsystems—social, technical, and administrative. A great deal of attention is also being given to examining organizations not as a complex of subsystems, but as units with their own cultures or as subcultural units within the larger societal culture. The various writings on the subject suggest that an organization's culture to a large extent may determine whether the organization succeeds or fails. The following list contains what some researchers believe are key features and effects of organizational culture:

1. Organizational culture affects employee productivity, job satisfaction, and commitment (Ouchi, 1981).
2. Organizational culture constrains organizational strategy and policy (Schwartz and Davis, 1981).
3. Groups in organizations often resist changes in their cultures (Dyer, 1982; Schwartz and Davis, 1981).
4. Conflicts between departments or conflicts accompanying mergers are caused by different cultures (Lawrence and Lorsch, 1967; Daughen and Binzen, 1971).
5. New recruits must learn the company culture to become accepted members of the organization (Van Maanen and Schein, 1979).
6. The field of organization development is devoted to making positive changes in the cultures of organizations (French and Bell, 1978).

These views indicate that organizational culture is a key variable in organizational analysis that must be considered by those interested in managing change effectively. This chapter will attempt to define the concept of organizational culture; describe how organizational cultures develop;

* This chapter by W. Gibb Dyer, Jr.: "I would like to acknowledge the contribution of William G. Dyer in formulating the ideas concerning implications for cultural change that appear at the end of this chapter. I would also like to thank Edgar H. Schein and Richard Beckhard for their helpful comments. This chapter was prepared with the support of: Chief of Naval Research, Psychological Sciences Division (Code 452), Organizational Effectiveness Research, Office of Naval Research, Arlington, VA 22247, under Contract #N00 4-80-0905: NR 170-911."

present a rudimentary framework for mapping culture; and, finally, present a few implications for managing culture change.

# What is Organizational Culture?

When anthropologists study a culture, they usually begin by examining physical artifacts, the language of the "natives," and various behavioral patterns. Similarly, students of organizational culture have focused on what might be called the verbal, behavioral, and physical "artifacts" exhibited by members of an organization (Schein, 1981). Verbal artifacts are socially shared languages, stories, and myths; behavioral artifacts are found in the organization's rituals, ceremonies, and behavior patterns; and physical artifacts are reflected in the organization's art, physical environment, and technology. Although these artifacts often have important symbolic meaning for members of an organization, they are merely the overt expressions of key *perspectives, values,* and *assumptions.* These perspectives, values, and assumptions are central because they embody the interpretation of the artifacts; they represent the belief system behind the artifacts. To explain this more clearly, let us briefly examine each of these aspects of culture and describe how they relate to one another.

## Perspectives

Perspectives are those socially shared ideas and actions used by members of an organization to deal with problematic situations. The situations to which these situation-specific rules of conduct are applied differ in their degree of concreteness, ranging from rather specific problems such as how to greet the boss first thing in the morning to more general issues such as how to advance to a top management position. Furthermore, perspectives entail both the formal and informal rules that a member of the organization uses to guide his or her behavior in relevant situations. One way to identify a "perspective" is to pose a problem. For example, a new member of an organization might ask: "What gets a person fired or in trouble around here?" or "How should an employee handle the performance review interview?" Depending on the organization, the answers to these kinds of questions often vary greatly and thus reflect rather different organizational cultures.

## Values

While perspectives prescribe appropriate conduct in a specific situation, values are broader, transsituational principles regarding the "goodness" or "badness" of particular artifacts and ideas. Values are the general goals, ideals, and "sins" of the organization. Leaders often attempt to formalize these broad standards in statements of "corporate philosophy" to provide general guidelines for individual organizational action. For example, one organization's statement of values specifies that the organization wants to be profitable; it wants to provide growth for its employees; it wants to protect the environment; it wants to make a quality product; and it wants employees to be ethical in their business dealings.

## Assumptions

The term "assumptions" refers to those taken-for-granted beliefs that are at the core of an organization's culture. They are the tacit premises from which the artifacts, perspectives, and values are derived. Perspectives and values may be somewhat similar in different organizations, but the basic organizational assumptions often are different; that is why some organizations are quite different from one another. It is not always easy to differentiate between an assumption and a value, both of which represent ways of looking at the culture and illustrate the way people act, feel, and think in the organization. The following example from the GEM Corporation illustrates how assumptions underlie the other "levels" of culture.

The relationships between each level of organizational culture is shown in Table 20.1, which is based on a "verbal artifact" from the GEM Cor-

### TABLE 20.1
### Levels of Organizational Culture

| | |
|---|---|
| **Culture Artifact** (*shared story*) | "There's the phrase: 'do what's right' . . . I was told a story when I first was coming aboard that described it. A middle manager who wanted to do something was told by his boss: 'No, you can't do that, that's crazy.' And so he pushed back. He did what was right. He went to the next guy up, his functional boss, and was told that it was crazy. So he went to the vice-president's level and they told him it was crazy, but 'do what's right.' And then he wound up in the president's office, and he was told it was crazy, but 'do what's right.' A piece of the culture says if it's right, you do it." |
| **Perspective** | Managers should show initiative—don't take no for an answer if you believe something is "right." Superiors shouldn't stifle this initiative. |
| **Value** | Autonomy is an important value in management. |
| **Basic Assumption** | Humans are basically good and capable of governing themselves. |

poration: a shared story about how a new manager was told to "do the right thing" to implement his idea. The story reflects a situation-specific perspective; that is, managers should stand firm even when ideas are rejected, and supervisors who encounter a subordinate with a "crazy idea" should not attempt to stifle his or her initiative. This story, together with GEM's socialization practice of leaving newcomers "alone" and GEM managers' "fear of rules and red tape," demonstrates the value of "autonomy" that is often discussed at GEM. After mapping a number of GEM values such as autonomy, we infer that a basic assumption underlying GEM culture is that humans are basically good and capable of governing themselves." This particular assumption has given rise to a vast array of artifacts, perspectives, and values. It is the theme that underlies the pieces of the GEM cultural mosaic and ties them together.

## Categories of Assumptions

Those who have studied organizational cultures have outlined several categories of assumptions that may prove useful (Kluckhohn and Strodtbeck, 1961; Schein, 1981). Table 20.2 lists six categories and briefly de-

---

### TABLE 20.2
### Categories of Assumptions

1. *The Nature of Relationships.* Are relationships between members of the organization assumed to be primarily hierarchical, collateral, or individualistic in nature?

2. *Human Nature.* Are humans considered to be basically good, basically evil, or neither good nor evil?

3. *The Nature of Truth.* Is "truth" (i.e., correct decisions) revealed by external authority figures, or is it determined by a process of personal investigation and testing?

4. *The Environment.* Is there a basic belief that humans can master the environment; or be subjugated by the environment; or attempt to harmonize with the environment?

5. *Assumptions about Time.* Are members of the organization primarily oriented to the past, the present, or the future?

6. *Assumptions about Activity.* Assumptions about the nature of human activity can be divided into three approaches:
   a. "Doing" orientation—Are humans basically active?
   b. "Being" orientation—Are humans passive and unable to alter existing circumstances?
   c. "Being" in becoming—Is a person's primary goal the development of self as an integrated whole?

---

scribes, in question form, the various orientations within a given category that might be found in a particular organizational culture.

Students of the field of management and organization studies will notice striking similarities between some of these categories and the ideas of other organizational theorists. For example, McGregor's Theory X and Theory Y assumptions closely parallel the assumptions raised here about human nature; the "nature of truth" assumptions are often implicit in the decision-making literature on participation (e.g., authoritarian vs. participative); the assumptions about the nature of activity appear often in the works of Maslow and Argyris; the assumptions about the environment reflect the theories of environmental orientations described by Miles and Snow (1978).

## Cultural Patterns

Within the framework of organizational culture, the "cultural pattern" is based upon the relationship between the prevailing core assumptions at a particular point in time. For example, a study of the culture of the GEM Corporation conducted by the author revealed three key assumptions:

1. Relationships are assumed to be reciprocal with strong bonds of kin-ship—like a "family."
2. Humans are assumed to be good and capable of governing themselves.
3. Truth is discovered through conflict, confrontation, and testing of ideas.

This particular pattern of assumptions underlies a culture that values autonomy and conflict while maintaining a supportive atmosphere through its strong kinship ties. Much like siblings, GEM employees "fight" with one another yet maintain close personal relationships. Moreover, their strong sense of individual initative fosters the confrontive, combative atmosphere.

In contrast, in the culture of another organization that the author has studied, relationships are primarily hierarchically ordered rather than reciprocal. People are assumed to be untrustworthy; truth is considered inherent in bureaucratic rules and regulations rather than discovered through conflict. The behavior of employees in this organization is characterized by careful conformity to company rules and the wishes of those in authority.

In summary, the key to understanding a culture lies in the particular patterning of the organization's core assumptions.

## "Creating Culture"

Having defined organizational culture, we will consider how organizational cultures are created and develop. It has been noted that individuals bring to an organization their own set of perspectives, values, and assumptions, and that this "latent culture" often determines their behavior in the organization. Although culture is, of course, a social and not an individual phenomenon, organizational founders/leaders create organizational cultures to the extent that they are able to impose their own beliefs on their subordinates.

Pettigrew (1979) points out that founders and other leaders "may be seen . . . as creators of symbols, ideologies, languages, beliefs, rituals and myths; aspects of the more cultural and expressive components of organizational life." Thus, one determinant of culture may reside in the particular set of perspectives, values, and assumptions that key organizational members bring to the workplace.

According to Edgar Schein, founders/leaders must solve two basic problems:

1. *Adapting* to the external environment.
2. *Integrating* members of the organization to work together in a cooperative effort.

Schein argues that organizational cultures emerge through attempts to solve these basic problems. A given "solution" that is deemed successful and valid by members of the organization reflects their shared understanding and thus forms the basis of cultural perspectives, values, and assumptions (Schein, 1981).

Another determinant of organizational culture may be found in the adaptive responses of individuals. Schein (1969) describes four basic problems individuals face when entering a group:

1. *Identify:* "Who am I to be?"
2. *Control and influence:* "Will I be able to control and influence others?"
3. *Needs and goals:* "Will the group goals include my own needs?"
4. *Acceptance:* "Will I be liked and accepted by the group?"

Individual solutions to these problems may be many and varied. If individual solutions that are not necessarily consistent with the prevailing culture are deemed useful by other members of the organization, they may be adopted and transmitted to succeeding generations. In this way, the cultural pattern may be changed or elaborated as "cultural innovation" takes place.

In summary, current theories of "culture creation" in organizations suggest that:

1. Organization founders or other leaders bring a culture to the workplace that is adopted by other members of the organization;
2. The assumptions, values, and perspectives of a given culture emerge as members of the organization attempt to solve the organizational problems of external adaptation and internal integration; and

3. Individual members of an organization may become "culture creators" by developing successful solutions to the problems of identity, control, individual needs, and acceptance, the solutions passed on to the next generation.

## Uncovering (Mapping) Organizational Cultures

To bring about change in an organization's culture, one must first uncover the existing cultural pattern. Following are some of the areas to examine and questions to ask.

As mentioned earlier, founders are often the source of an organization's culture. Thus, it is useful to learn:

1. Why was the organization founded? What was the founder/leader trying to achieve?
2. What problems did the founder/leader encounter in managing the business? How were they solved?
3. What are the founder's/leader's perspectives, values, and assumptions concerning how the organization should be managed?

Organizational responses to the problems of adaptation and integration may be discovered by determining:

1. What major crises has the organization confronted? How did the organization deal with these crises?
2. What major changes have been made?
    a. Strategy
    b. Structure
    c. Technology
    d. Organizational Size
    e. Leadership
    How and why were the changes made? How did these changes affect the organization?
3. How does the organization reward and control its members?
4. How are decisions made; e.g., participative vs. authoritarian?
5. What are relations between employees; e.g., close vs. individualistic?

To determine individual adaptation responses, one might ask:

1. What are the organization's socialization practices?
2. What does an employee need to know or do to become an accepted member of the organization?
3. Which individuals have been successful and which have failed? Why?
4. How does one gain power and influence?
5. How do some get "noticed" and get their ideas adopted?

Of course, these questions are not comprehensive. The change agent should develop questions and hypotheses about the culture during the analysis.

To begin to answer these questions, one might obtain data from the following sources:

1. Key inside informants—The analyst should attempt to find informants who are knowledgeable about the organization.
2. Outside informants—Similarly, interviews might be conducted with customers, suppliers, external consultants, etc.
3. Observation—If possible, the analyst should observe and participate in activities of the group under investigation to obtain first-hand accounts of social scenes of interest.
4. Internal documents—Annual reports, histories, memos, and operational data are useful to corroborate and expand on data gathered from interviews and observations.
5. External documents—Industry publications, newspaper reports, and other external reports also can be invaluable sources of information.
6. Questionnaires—Although questionnaires are of limited benefit in mapping a culture, they can be useful to test hypotheses or gather attitudinal data after a preliminary study has been completed.

At this point, a few notes of caution are in order, First, the analyst is not likely to find a single organizational culture but, rather, multiple cultures, usually along department or hierarchical boundaries. Thus, one must attempt to delineate different perspectives, values, and assumptions and outline the boundaries and "overlaps" between cultures that may be embedded in the organization. Second, because discrepancies between espoused beliefs and actual behavior are commonplace, it is necessary to differentiate the espoused or ideal culture from the practices of members of the organization. The change agent should attempt to discover under what conditions organizational members deviate from espoused beliefs. Finally, cultural studies are often difficult to disguise. Care must be taken to protect informants as well as the organization itself, if one agrees to keep findings anonymous.

## Managing Cultural Change

The process of managing cultural change in organizations is relatively unexplored terrain, even though the field of organization development purports to address the creation of positive change. Burke (1983) defines organization development as being devoted to "culture change." The following seven steps incorporate the key activities and processes that accompany successful efforts to manage cultural change:

## 1. *Conduct a Culture Audit*

The first step in the change process involves a diagnosis of the culture. Crucial perspectives, values and assumptions shared by members of the organization, and of potential subcultures within the organizations, should be mapped out, and key situations and activities in which the culture is "played out" should be delineated. Discrepancies between espoused beliefs and actual behavior also should be noted. The goal of the diagnosis is to develop an accurate "map" of the cultural pattern.

## 2. *Cultural Assessment and Need for Change*

After the cultural pattern is outlined, the effects of the pattern can be assessed and the need for change determined. Cultural change is often needed if 1) the cultural pattern is not solving or will not solve problems of integration or adaptation; or 2) the pattern has negative consequences for individuals in the organization. For example, as organizations grow and evolve, their cultures may become incompatible with the changing circumstances. Particular values and beliefs that were highly functional when a company was small may prove dysfunctional after significant growth. Similarly, cultural conditions can cause high turnover. In assessing the need for change, it is critical to determine the causal links between the cultural pattern and current problems facing the organization, and to recognize that problems, including those of a technological or structural nature, do not necessarily arise from the culture.

## 3. *Assess Cultural Risk*

If a proposed change violates current cultural values and assumptions, managing the change may be exceedingly difficult. Thus, one must assess the risk of failure as well as explore potential negative consequences of a given change (Schwartz and Davis, 1983). If a change is consistent with the prevailing culture, success is more likely. For example, attempting to change a culture that values autonomy into one that values hierarchical authority would probably be quite difficult. However, if a culture that values conflict, like the GEM Corporation, was to adopt use of a structured conflict decision-making model such as the Delphi technique, the change might be readily acceptable because this model operates on the premise that conflict is desirable. In this way, the potential risk of any intervention can be assessed by examining its congruence or incongruence with the prevailing cultural pattern. Moreover, any change in one of the key assumptions or values may affect the rest of the pattern; one must weigh the risk of changing desirable aspects of the culture along with undesirable ones.

## 4. Unfreezing the Cultural Pattern

Kurt Lewin has suggested that change occurs only after a system is "unfrozen." In the case of organizational culture, this means when the underlying perspectives, values, and/or assumptions are called into question, thereby producing a high degree of tension.

We have characterized culture primarily in terms of basic assumptions—fundamental beliefs about human nature, the environment, etc. Because these tacit premises are rarely questioned, they are not easily changed. Indeed, several studies of organizational culture indicate that cultural changes generally are *not* planned, but accompany sudden, and at times cataclysmic, events such as:

1. Death or retirement of the founder/leader.
2. Leadership succession.
3. A decision to merge or sell the business.
4. Dramatic changes in growth or profitability.
5. Major technological changes.
6. Fundamental changes in strategy and/or structure.

These events often "unfreeze" or destabilize the entire cultural "system," causing various previously predictable behaviors to become unpredictable. A change agent might explore the extent to which members of the organization can anticipate such events and capitalize on the opportunities to initiate cultural changes.

Although cultural change may be possible in the absence of such dramatic events, fundamental changes probably will not occur unless the cultural pattern is somehow destabilized. Thus, the change agent may require a certain opportunism to begin the change process when such events occur or to create conditions that may unfreeze the pattern.

## 5. Elicit Support from the Cultural Elite

Top management or other opinion leaders often compose the "cultural elite" in the organization. As "culture setters," they interpret events for members of the organization and establish the rules of conduct. Because successful cultural change may be impossible without the assistance of these individuals, a strategy for locating them and generating their support is essential.

## 6. Selection and Intervention Strategy

Once the previous steps have been followed, interventions for carrying out change can be developed and implemented. Although a variety of interventions are possible, cultural change usually occurs when people adopt a different set of values and assumptions. Reorientation of new and old employees to the new cultural pattern may require extensive training, new reward systems, and new structures. Team-building, role negotiation, bargaining interventions, and the replacement of key individuals who hold the "old" beliefs may be necessary.

### 7. Monitoring and Evaluation

Culture change is characterized by incremental changes over time and rarely occurs quickly. Thus, a system for monitoring and evaluating the transition to a new set of values and beliefs is essential for the development of new strategies and interventions.

## Implications for Creating Culture Change

Changing an organization's culture is considerably more dramatic than modifying parts of a system. From a systems point of view, the focus of change usually is the improvement of certain system outputs through modifications in subsystem conditions. But at the deepest level, a cultural change requires alteration of the basic assumptions of the organization and its essential character.

According to this analysis, there is a flow between assumptions → values → perspectives → artifacts. The values, perspectives, and artifacts are natural consequences of the pattern of assumptions. Given this view, is the process reversible? Does changing the artifacts, rules, regulations, or definitions of behavior result in a shift in values or assumptions? At least one reverse flow occurs when new rules or even physical changes are initiated by a strong new leader. As noted, leadership succession has a major impact on an organization's culture; a new leader with different assumptions and values has great potential for altering the prevailing pattern of culture. Business history is replete with stories of cultures formed by organizational founders such as Henry Ford, John D. Rockefeller, Thomas Watson, Andrew Carnegie, Hewlett and Packard, J. C. Penney, and Willard Marriot, to name just a few. More recent anecdotal evidence supports the notion that a strong new leader, such as Lee Iacocca at Chrysler and Charles Brown at AT&T, can have an impact on the culture of the total organization.

Early in the study of organizations, Max Weber wrestled with the issues surrounding fundamental change in organizations that have become routinized and bureaucratized. He theorized that a "charismatic" leader, whom others perceive as having extraordinary powers, would be able to shift the basic pattern of an organization. From a position of power and influence, the new leader could articulate new patterns and values that would be accepted (although not always without resistance and conflict). Weber points out the charismatic power of Jesus Christ, who preached a new set of beliefs and warned of the ineffectiveness of trying to piece together the old and new cultures; the resulting conflict between the old and new forces led to his crucifixion. Michals's provocative "Iron Law of the Oligarchy" suggests that when the charismatic leader is gone, his or her strong lieutenants or disciples (the oligarchy) attempt to establish and perpetuate the leader's cultural pattern. This pattern remains until a new charismatic leader emerges and another round of change occurs.

More recently, Robert Guest's study of an automotive plant demonstrates how the basic cultural pattern changed when the plant manager was replaced. The new manager held different assumptions about the nature of the workers, the way people should be treated, and the processes for getting decisions made and work accomplished (Guest, 1962).

In altering an organization's culture by initiating a change in leadership, one must seek certain qualities: 1) the new leader must have personal charisma or organizational power; 2) the new leader must hold basic assumptions and values necessary to replace the old ones; 3) the new leader requires skill in relating to others; 4) the new leader must articulate the new pattern and implement the perspectives (rules, regulations) and artifacts that represent the new pattern; and 5) the leader must be able to manage resistance in such a way that conflict does not cripple the organizations.

Another change strategy involves changing the basic assumptions and values of existing leaders so that they become catalysts for initiating broader changes in the organization's culture. This strategy was integral to the T-group, sensitivity training movement that was the predominant management training mode during the 1950s and 1960s, when McGregor, Likert, Blake, and Mouton were writing about the desirability of the Theory Y, System 4, and 9-9 styles of leadership. At that time, the answer to the inevitable question, "How do you change an organization from Theory X to Theory Y or from System One to System Four or from 9-1 to 9-9?" was to send key managers to a T-group. However, research regarding the impact of T-group training on basic organizational cultural patterns is not encouraging. There were indications that graduates of T-groups did alter some personal behavior patterns, but it is not clear how much they affected basic values and assumptions in the organization. In response to the relative ineffectiveness of T-groups in making organizationwide changes, a new movement called Organization Development (O.D.) addressed the alteration of organization structures and processes with less emphasis on changing the basic values of the existing leaders. There is little evidence that O.D. interventions result in change in the basic assumptions of the organization. Many organization development professionals hold cultural values different than the prevailing culture of the organizations they work in, but their interventions are often geared to altering system conditions or processes rather than producing deeper cultural change.

An organization development intervention may result in change in an existing procedure, policy, regulation, behavioral pattern, or the restructuring or enlargement of a job. At one level, this represents a change in the culture, but certain of the artifacts and perspectives of a culture nevertheless can be changed without disturbing the basic assumptions or values to any great degree. Although workers in the system, see that some conditions have changed, the fundamental character of the organization remains the same. The critical issue is still, "How important is a change in basic assumptions and values in effecting any real change at any level, and how do you bring about these basic changes in the culture?"

## Summary

Organizational culture and culture change are exciting and largely unexplored areas of interest in the field of organization development. It is hoped that the information presented in this chapter will provide new ideas and tools with which to better understand and manage the process of culture change in organizations.

# CHAPTER 21

# Improving Creativity in Organizations

Although creativity has been given a great deal of attention over the past twenty years, most research has focused on identifying individual creative forces, discovering factors correlated with creativity, and measuring creativity in individuals. There has been little investigation of the organizational conditions that foster and release creativity in employees, and even less attention has been paid to the management process; no one has adequately answered such questions as, "How do you manage people in a way that either promotes or inhibits creative behavior?" Most organizational change efforts have centered on boosting productivity, increasing morale, or reducing conflict rather than improving the level of creativity or innovation.

## Creativity and Organizational Development

Over twenty-five years ago in Great Britain, Burns and Stalker identified two different styles of management whose success depended on the nature of the basic task or production process of the organization. The "mechanistic" style—a restrictive, mechanical, rules-and-regulations style—was effective in work settings such as the textile industry, in which tasks were routine and unchanging. The "organic" style, which was found in electronic firms, was characterized by more freedom, less observation, fewer rules and routines. The "organic" situations required more innovation and creativity because of marketplace demands for new products, devices, and designs.

The need for creativity is affected by the nature of the organization. Some organizations should constantly encourage innovation, while other organizations have less need for new or fresh ideas. A basic problem exists in an organization that needs imagination but stifles it, or that hires creative people but can and does function successfully the old way. In one case creative people are blocked, and in the other case creative people feel useless or unwanted.

To meet the need for a consistent flow of new products, many organizations have established research and development units specifically to generate new product ideas. Current studies of the management of such units are addressing these questions: Does an R&D manager manage in the same way as one would in a sales, manufacturing, marketing, or financial unit? To what extent do different activities require different management styles and orientations? Do creative people require new and different styles and behaviors in their superiors?

Aside from their need for creative products or services, almost all organizations confront a range of decisions and actions that would benefit from a more imaginative and creative approach. For example, most business organizations could successfully employ more imagination in developing new markets, new sales methods, new uses of equipment, and new solutions to personnel and administrative problems.

Almost all areas of any organization could profit from the ability to devise more creative solutions to problems. Yet one of the major current dilemmas in organization development is the possibility that change efforts are antithetical to the release of creativity. Many development activities begin with team-building, which emphasizes a climate of trust and openness in which people can relate more authentically with one another and through which a sense of cohesion and identity can be fostered in the work unit. Team-building often addresses group functions such as decision making by consensus and achieving interdependence in effective team efforts.

Although team development may be vitally needed in some organizations, is it universally required? If we emphasize collaboration, consensus decision-making, cohesion, interdependence, and work units that meet social needs for inclusion, warmth, and connectedness, to what extent do we inhibit organizational creativity? Too little attention has been directed at the side effects of an organizational change effort that emphasizes collaboration.

## The Creative Individual

In the literature on creativity, evidence is ample that the highly creative person is a nonconformist in many ways (see Table 21.1). How much do current organization development efforts, which stress integration and, to some extent, conformity and cohesion, restrict and inhibit the highly individualistic, somewhat unorthodox creative person? If we maximize the importance of the cohesive work unit, do we simultaneously suppress the creative process that might unleash innovative potential in work unit members?

The Barron summary of the creative individual includes behavioral characteristics that are often incompatible with a collaborative organizational model. Change plans in many organizations incorporate too many controls to accommodate such people.

## TABLE 21.1
## Research Summary of Characteristics of the
## Creative Individual*

I. Traits seen in perceptual habits
    A. Tolerance of ambiguity (can live with areas of confusion)
        1. Preference for complexity in phenomena
        2. Preference for imbalance in phenomena
        3. Openness to variety in phenomena
    B. Breadth of interest
    C. Perceptual control
        1. Flexibility
        2. Deferment of judgment

II. Traits seen in awareness of self
    A. Personal complexity
    B. Rejection of suppression as a means of controlling impulse
    C. Immediacy of response to stimuli

III. Traits seen in interaction with others
    A. Self-assertion; tendency to dominate through drive
    B. Verbal fluency
    C. Impulsiveness
    D. Expansiveness
    E. Nonconformity
    F. Tendency to release tension readily through motor activity
    G. Independence of judgment

IV. Traits seen in motivation
    A. Rapid personal tempo
    B. High level of drive

V. Traits in relation to others
    A. Not a joiner, has few close friends
    B. Relatively little interest in interpersonal relations
    C. Independence from parents

VI. Traits in job attitudes
    A. Preference for things and ideas to people
    B. High regard for intellectual interests
    C. Less emphasis on and value in job security
    D. Less enjoyment in and satisfaction from detail work and routine
    E. High level of resourcefulness and adaptability
    F. Scepticism
    G. Precision and critical ability; honesty
    H. Persistence

VII. Other traits
    A. Spontaneity
    B. Stubbornness
    C. Adventurousness
    D. Anxiety

*Adapted from Barron (1969).

## TABLE 21.2
### Comparison of the Creative Individual
### and the Creative Organization*

| The Creative Individual | The Creative Organization |
| --- | --- |
| **A.** Conceptual fluency; is able to produce a large number of ideas quickly | **A.** Has idea people, open channels of communication, and ad hoc devices, such as suggestion systems, brainstorming, and idea units absolved of other responsibilities; encourages contact with outside sources. |
| **B.** Originality; generates unusual ideas | **B.** Heterogeneous personnel policy; includes marginal, unusual types; assigns nonspecialists to problems; allows eccentricity. |
| **C.** Separates source from content in evaluating information; is motivated by interest in problem; follows wherever it leads | **C.** Has an objective, fact-founded approach; ideas evaluated on their merits, not on status of originator; has ad hoc approaches, such as anonymous communications and blind votes; selects and promotes on merit only |
| **D.** Suspends judgment; avoids early commitment; spends more time in analysis; exploration | **D.** Has financial, material commitment to products, policies; invests in basic research; uses flexible, long-range planning; experiments with new ideas rather than prejudging on "rational" grounds; everything gets a chance |
| **E.** Less authoritarian; has relativistic view of life | **E.** More decentralized, diversified; administrative slack, time, and resources to absorb errors; risk-taking ethos; tolerates and expects taking chances |
| **F.** Accepts own impulses; playful; undisciplined exploration | **F.** Not run as "tight ship"; employees have fun; allows freedom to choose and pursue problems and freedom to discuss ideas |
| **G.** Independence of judgment; less conformity | **G.** Organizationally autonomous |
| **H.** Deviant, sees self as different | **H.** Original and different objectives, not trying to be another "X" |

*Table 21.2 continued*

| | |
|---|---|
| **I.** Rich, "bizarre" fantasy life and superior reality orientation; controls | **I.** Security of routine; allows innovation; "Philistines" provide stable, secure environment that allows "creators" to roam |

*Adapted from Steiner (1965).

## Creative Organizations and Management

Only recently have researchers examined conditions characteristic of highly creative or innovative organizations (Galbraith, 1982). Table 21.2, which compares the creative individual and the creative organization, shows that certain conditions in the current organizational change framework also are present in the creative organization. However, there are additional conditions in the creative organization that, up to now at least, have not been generally considered important in organization development. For example, the creative organization encourages unusual types of people. It allows eccentricity. It employs a range of unique ad hoc devices to encourage freethinking and new ideas, such as a game room and play equipment. It sets up norms for risk-taking and tolerates the new and the unexpected. It provides a fun-loving atmosphere and freedom to pursue ideas not in the organizational mainstream.

If we want to enhance creativity, how do we train managers to establish these conditions rather than conditions that at present seem to pay off more in the organizational system? Most managers are rewarded if their unit operates efficiently and effectively. A highly creative unit, in contrast, might appear ineffective and uneven and rather crazy to an outside or inside observer. Can an organization tolerate that? Can we reward managers who can produce conditions contrary to the mainstream of current organizational thinking?

Table 21.3, Encouragement of Creativity through Management and Organization, identifies management and organization conditions that release or inhibit people's creative actions. By completing the scale, one may identify areas where change may be needed.

One research study identified thirteen conditions considered unfavorable and five conditions considered favorable for creative and productive work in science. The unfavorable conditions mentioned most frequently by scientists interviewed were instability of the budget; conflict between the demands of management activities and research activities; inadequacies in supportive groups and procedures; inadequacies in compensation and other attractions; lack of professional internship for young scientists; poor communications with scientists working elsewhere on related prob-

## TABLE 21.3
## Encouragement of Creativity Through
## Management and Organization*

*This scale will help you see to what extent the type of management and the organizational conditions support and encourage creative effort.*

| Conditions Discouraging Creativity | | Conditions Encouraging Creativity |
|---|---|---|
| 1. My ideas or suggestions never get a fair hearing. | 1 2 3 4 5 6 7 | My ideas or suggestions get a fair hearing. |
| 2. I feel that my boss is not interested in my ideas. | 1 2 3 4 5 6 7 | I feel that my boss is very much interested in my ideas. |
| 3. I receive no encouragement to innovate on my job. | 1 2 3 4 5 6 7 | I am encouraged to innovate on my job. |
| 4. There is no reward for innovating or improving things on my job. | 1 2 3 4 5 6 7 | I am rewarded for innovating and improving on my job. |
| 5. There is no encouragement for diverse opinions among subordinates. | 1 2 3 4 5 6 7 | There is encouragement of diversity of opinion among subordinates. |
| 6. I'm very reluctant to tell my boss about mistakes I make. | 1 2 3 4 5 6 7 | I feel comfortable enough with my boss to tell him about mistakes I make. |
| 7. I'm not given enough responsibility for me to do my job right. | 1 2 3 4 5 6 7 | I am given enough responsibility for me to do my job right. |
| 8. To really succeed in this organization, one needs to be a friend or a relative of the boss. | 1 2 3 4 5 6 7 | There is no favoritism in the organization. |
| 9. There are other jobs in this organization that I would prefer to have. | 1 2 3 4 5 6 7 | I have the job in this organization that I think I do best. |
| 10. They keep close watch over me too much of the time. | 1 2 3 4 5 6 7 | They trust me to do my job without always checking on me. |
| 11. They would not let me try other jobs in the organization. | 1 2 3 4 5 6 7 | I could try other kinds of jobs in the organization if I wanted to. |

*Table 21.3 continued*

| | | |
|---|---|---|
| **12.** The management is made very uptight by confusion, disorder, and chaos. | 1 2 3 4 5 6 7 | The management deals easily with confusion, disorder, and chaos. |
| **13.** There is a low standard of excellence on the job. | 1 2 3 4 5 6 7 | There is a high standard of excellence for me on the job. |
| **14.** My boss is not open to receive my opinion about how he might improve his own performance on the job. | 1 2 3 4 5 6 7 | My boss is very open to suggestions on how he might improve his own performance. |
| **15.** My boss has a very low standard for judging his own performance. | 1 2 3 4 5 6 7 | My boss has a very high standard of excellence for judging his own performance. |
| **16.** I am not asked for suggestions on how to improve service to the customers. | 1 2 3 4 5 6 7 | The management actively solicits my suggestions and ideas on how to improve the service to customers. |
| **17.** My boss shows no enthusiasm for the work in which we are engaged. | 1 2 3 4 5 6 7 | My boss exhibits a lot of enthusiasm for the work in which we are engaged. |
| **18.** Mistakes get you in trouble; they aren't to learn from. | 1 2 3 4 5 6 7 | Around here mistakes are to learn from and not to penalize you. |
| **19.** Someone else dictates how much I should accomplish on my job. | 1 2 3 4 5 6 7 | I'm allowed to set my own goals for my job. |
| **20.** I am very much dissatisfied with my job. | 1 2 3 4 5 6 7 | I am very much satisfied with my job. |
| **21.** My boss never lets me know how I stand with him. | 1 2 3 4 5 6 7 | My boss keeps me informed on how I stand with him. |
| **22.** My boss does not communicate clearly what I am to do. | 1 2 3 4 5 6 7 | My boss communicates clearly what I am supposed to do. |
| **23.** The organization has too many rules and regulations for me. | 1 2 3 4 5 6 7 | The organization has adequate rules and regulations for me. |

*With Philip B. Daniels.

lems; inadequacy of physical facilities; dearth of suitable recognition; exclusion of scientists from high-level decision-making on scientific problems; insufficient long-range planning in the total scientific program; interference between monitoring and regular research activities; inefficiency in selection and placement programs; and lack of personal counseling for scientists. The favorable conditions included individual freedoms, the intellectual challenge of the work, location and certain facilities, relative stability of employment, and encouragement of continual training. Those interested in improving creativity in organizations should examine these conditions carefully.

# Training for Organizational Creativity

Can a creative person become an effective manager? Should we seek a creative person for a management position or seek a manager with the ability to manage creative people although he himself may not be particularly creative? Current management-training methods do not reward the highly individualistic, nonconforming, creative person. Very little emphasis has been placed on the ability to guide and stimulate the creative efforts of others. In a typical management-development program with an experience-based focus, it is common to see the nonconformist, the rebel, the individualistically oriented person with deviant behaviors and peculiar idiosyncrasies subjected to initial negative reactions and negative feedback. Such a person would learn through this kind of training experience that the best way to get along with others is to conform to their expectations. If he can identify the group norms and modify his behavior to suit those norms, he will experience the warmth, acceptance, and rewards of the group. Perhaps these conditions should not be emphasized if we are to encourage the creative person or train managers to work effectively with creative people or release the creative potential of others. It is possible to develop a training process that emphasizes a set of norms entirely different from the ones mentioned above. Using the same methodology, a whole new set of behaviors could be identified and encouraged in management-development programs.

## The Need for Innovation

It seems apparent that some organizations do not need more trust, increased collaboration, better relationships, or even greater effort. In these productive, contented organizations, the major deficiency is that the people and their programs are in a rut, doing the same things the same way even though conditions and problems have changed. For some reason, new ideas, new solutions to problems, new services, new organization forms, procedures, or processes are not encouraged or fostered. Such an organization could improve its effectiveness through an effort to stimulate innovation and find more interesting and stimulating ways to function, solve problems, render services, or improve the product. This would require a form of development quite different from a developmental program for an organization bogged down in conflict, rivalry, suspicion, and low trust.

## The Innovative Organization

Galbraith (1982) has identified three individuals who are crucial if innovation is to occur and move to fruition in an organization. First is the *idea generator*—the creative person. Next comes the *sponsor,* who is in a position of influence and can promote the idea generator's creative contribution; without a sponsor, many creative ideas are stalled. Third is the *orchestrator,* who understands the system's political processes and can organize the funding and support and put the idea into production. These three roles are usually not taken by the same person. All three roles should be supported and encouraged with incentives.

## Management Actions that Foster Creativity

Steiner (1965) has identified five management behaviors that encourage the development of creativity:

*1. Values and rewards.* The creative organization prizes and rewards creativity. A management philosophy that stresses creativity as an organizational goal, that encourages and expects it at all levels, will increase the chances of its occurrence.

*2. Compensation.* It is probably this simple: Where creativity and not productivity is the goal, creativity and not productivity should be measured and rewarded.

*3. Channels for advancement.* To the extent possible, there should be formal channels for advancement and status within creative areas.

*4. Freedom.* Within rather broad limits, creativity is increased by giving creators freedom in choice of project or problem and method of pursuit.

*5. Communication.* Many observers stress the importance of free and open channels of communication, both vertical and horizontal.

## Elements of a Development Program in Creativity

These elements are reminiscent of those discussed earlier.

*1. Assessment.* Through an instrument similar to the one in Table 21.3, the change agent can analyze the organization's current level of innovation and the employees' desire or need for more creative effort in their work.

**2.** *Action-planning.* The change agent next can use the assessment to develop a plan of action for stimulating innovation. Depending on the findings, he or she might recommend some of the following actions:

*a)* Hold seminars on creative thinking.
*b)* Offer a reward-bonus incentive program for productive new ideas.
*c)* Allow free time for individual or group creative problem-solving.
*d)* Arrange regular staff meetings in which people freewheel and brainstorm to create innovations.
*e)* Form new or unusual short-term groups to stimulate crossfertilization of ideas.
*f)* Equip a laboratory, workshop, or "think tank" with materials for tinkering, thinking, and planning.
*g)* Encourage performance reviews that inspire and support creative efforts, ideas, and actions.
*h)* Implement a policy that reduces fear of failure during experimentation.
*i)* Inform employees of problems in the organization that they might solve.
*j)* Develop a reward-and-recognition system for the creative person.
*k)* Recruit an outsider to assess creative output and suggest ways of improving innovation within the organization.
*l)* Hold a team-development session specifically to enhance the creative atmosphere and output of a department or unit.
*m)* Rotate employees into different positions or sections of the organization so that a new mixture of people can address old problems.
*n)* Hold a job-enrichment session in which people devise ways of enriching their own jobs.

**3.** *Implementing the plan.* After a plan of action has been developed, it must be put into operation. Employees must be willing to invest time and energy to ensure that new programs and actions have a fair chance to succeed.

**4.** *Assessing the plan.* After a new program has been functioning for a period of time, it must be evaluated to determine whether it is achieving the results desired. Interviews, questionnaires, group discussions, and reaction panels can indicate whether the new actions have indeed resulted in a more creative organizational climate, with an increase in the creative output of individuals and more imaginative solutions to problems.

# Implications for Managing Change

The issue of creativity or innovation has serious implications for those managing organizations and those planning changes in organizations.

Creativity is often at odds with the conditions that foster collaboration. It is possible to increase team work while inhibiting creativity, which seems to stem from the less fettered individual.

It is a critical challenge for the change team to undertake an in-depth assessment of the organization, concentrating on the need for creativity, before any change plan is devised. Innovation in organizations has been receiving a great deal of attention recently. Most research evidence indicates that it is easier to innovate in smaller organizations; creativity is lost as the system grows. In large organizations, a systematic plan is required for appointing people to appropriate roles and providing adequate incentives to stimulate greater innovation.

# CHAPTER 22

# Changing Dysfunctional Decisions*

If you were asked if your goal was to fail in any given venture, your response probably would be an indignant no—you would insist that your efforts were directed toward success. The fact remains that many people) cause their own defeat as surely as if they had made a conscious decision to fail. Change agents often try to alter the tendency in some individuals and organizations to engage in self-defeating activities. The following example illustrates this kind of failure-oriented behavior.

### The Trip to Abilene: A Modern Parable

A young man and his bride are visiting her folks in the town of Coleman, Texas, in the middle of the summer. Coleman is in the plains, and the wind blows, and it gets hot. There is not much to do in Coleman, a town of about five thousand people. The young man, his wife, and the parents-in-law are sitting around on a Sunday afternoon, drinking lemonade and playing dominoes, and, from all appearances, having a good time. Suddenly and surprisingly, the father-in-law says, "Why don't we all get dressed and drive to Abilene and have dinner in the cafeteria?"

The young man thinks to himself, "Good night! There is nothing I would like to do less than drive to Abilene." Abilene is fifty-three miles from Coleman, over a winding road. He knows that the automobile does not have air conditioning; in order to keep dust from blowing in, they will have to drive with the windows up. He also knows that the only place to eat on a Sunday afternoon is the Good Luck Cafeteria, where the food leaves much to be desired. But he thinks, "If my father-in-law wants to go to Abilene, I guess it's all right." So he says, "That sounds fine to me if Beth wants to go."

Beth says, "Well, yes, if everyone wants to go to Abilene, that's fine—if mother really wants to go."

Mother replies, "Oh, yes, if you all want to go, well, that's where I want to go."

They all put on their Sunday clothes, climb into the old Buick, and take a long, hot, dusty trip to Abilene. When they arrive, sure enough,

*This chapter was written with Jerry B. Harvey.

the only place open is the Good Luck Cafeteria. They have a greasy meal, crowd into the automobile, and drive fifty-three miles home.

Worn out, hot, tired, dirty, irritable, they finally struggle back into the house and have another glass of lemonade. The father-in-law says, "Boy, am I glad that's over! If there's anything I didn't want to do, it was go to Abilene. I sure wouldn't have gone if you three hadn't pressured me into it!"

The son-in-law says, "What do you mean, you didn't want to go to Abilene? And what do you mean, we pressured you into it? I only went because the rest of you wanted to go. I didn't pressure anybody."

His wife speaks up: "What do you mean? I didn't want to go to Abilene. The only reason I went was because you, mama, and daddy wanted to go."

Mother chimes in: "I didn't want to go to Abilene. That's the last place in the world I wanted to go. I only went because father and the two of you said you wanted to go."

Father expands on his previous statement, "As I said before, I didn't want to go to Abilene. I just suggested going because I was afraid everybody was really bored sitting around playing dominoes, and I thought you might prefer to do something else. I was just sort of making conversation, hoping you'd suggest something better, but I really didn't expect you to take me up on my idea."


And so we have an interesting paradox: four reasonably intelligent people agreeing to do something that none of them wanted to do in the first place. As a paradox within a paradox, this inability to cope with agreement (that is, the hidden agreement that they didn't want to go to Abilene) can be considered the basic cause of their dilemma.

This is a parable. As with any parable, there may be many interpretations and many lessons to be learned. You might observe a problem in communication. You might detect an element of fear. You might see love. It is also possible to draw conclusions about integrity. Of central concern is an action in which each of us individually and collectively may engage from time to time—that is, taking an unwanted trip to Abilene. In fact, one of the primary functions of effective management of families, churches, businesses, and governments is to keep people from taking a dusty trip to Abilene and eating a greasy meal at the Good Luck Cafeteria. There are many different kinds of trips to Abilene; following are just a few that occur at the personal, interpersonal, and organizational levels. In each case, the issue is the same—public decisions that people privately do not favor. An important goal for change for some people in some organizations is to understand that they make decisions they really do not want and to break out of this highly dysfunctional process.

# Personal Decisions to Fail

Some decisions to fail are made during critical life choices—for example, in choosing a life's companion. Consider a young man and a young woman who have been going together for some time and are planning to be married. If you were to interview each of them privately and ask, "How do you feel about this person you have selected?" they might answer something like this: "Honestly, now that you have asked, I really feel deep down that this isn't the right person. There are many things we don't share or understand or like about each other." Unfortunately, like many couples wanting to bolster a sagging relationship, they gave in to increasing demands for personal intimacy. Expectations built up among themselves, their families, and their friends until it became difficult—at least in their minds—to terminate the relationship. Both made the decision to marry, although neither really wants to or considers it the right thing to do. The girl thinks, "He is expecting to go through with this." The boy says to himself, "I am sure she is planning the wedding." If you ask them, "What are you going to do about this situation?" they will probably say, "We are going to announce our wedding date next week." This young couple is in danger of taking a tragic trip to Abilene by doing something that neither wants to do and by engaging in an activity and making a crucial decision that neither feels is appropriate. One might say they are making a decision to fail.

Another kind of trip to Abilene might involve choosing an occupation or a lifestyle. For example, you might ask a recent college graduate, "What do you want to do now that you have your degree?"

If he searched deep within himself, he might say, "You know, what I would really like to do is buy a farm, raise some cattle, teach high school, and work with the Boy Scouts."

"What are you going to do?"

"Well, next week I am going to Los Angeles to accept a job in the aerospace industry."

If he acts on this decision, he will for all intents and purposes consign himself to an endless series of meals at the Good Luck Cafeteria.

Not all students make such a poor choice. Recently, for instance, a graduate who had received an MBA degree wrote to his professor:

> I was contemplating traveling to any number of metropolitan areas to find work because my search at school left me jobless. Instead, I took a construction job in Grand Teton National Park with hopes of latching onto something in that area. At the summer's end I received an offer of a job in park management at Grand Teton. I have had a chance to think throughout the quiet winter evenings, and I realize that I am much happier than I would have been surrounded by the noise and bustle of city life. I have also come to realize that I was just not cut out for the keen competitive life of high finance and am

thoroughly enjoying the more leisurely approach in the National
Park Service. Living in an area that is only five miles from work and
less than fifty yards from the woods makes up for whatever might
be lacking in the way of culture and comfort.

Here is at least one young man who avoided a dusty trip to Abilene.

Not everyone need live on the farm or in the woods to avoid that
miserable trip. There are some who, if they were to search the deeper
recesses of their own minds, would say, "I really want to be a writer,"
or "I have the capacity to be a top-flight scientist. I really should get a
Ph.D." But their trip to Abilene involves taking the nearest, most available
job at the best salary. They are in danger of arriving at Abilene, a place
they don't want to be, and joining the fellows in the aerospace industry
for a greasy meal at the Good Luck Cafeteria.

## Interpersonal Decisions to Fail

Married couples may find themselves on the road to Abilene as they begin
to move in directions that neither really wants. If you were to talk to each
of them privately, the interviews would go something like this:

To the young wife, "How do you feel about your relationship?"

"I'm not satisfied or happy."

"What's the matter?"

"We don't do a lot of things together. We are drifting away from our
basic values. We tend to bicker and quarrel and fight with each other
more than we should."

"You're not satisfied with that?"

"No, I don't like it at all."

Likewise, if you talk with the young husband, you would probably
hear the same thing: "I don't like it. I'm not satisfied with what we are
doing. I don't really like the direction we are taking. It isn't what I want."

"What are you going to do about it?"

"Well, we'll probably sit in the front room and quarrel and fight, then
go to bed and sulk."

Such a couple is indeed taking a trip to Abilene, when Salt Lake City
or San Bernardino is where they would rather be.

In a striking piece of research in the field of social psychology, a professor at Yale, Stanley Milgram, described a dangerous kind of trip to
Abilene. To test his hypothesis that people relinquish their responsibility
for decisions to those in positions of authority, he invited college students
into a laboratory where they saw a man seated in what appeared to be
an electric chair with electrodes attached to his body (the students were
unaware that the chair was fake; it was not electrified.) The experimenter
announced, "We want to see how much electric shock affects a person's
ability to learn. Would you sit at the control board and manipulate a

central knob that will shock the person with increasing amounts of electricity?"

As each student sat, the experimenter instructed him or her to turn the switch, whereupon a light went on in front of the electric chair and the man in the chair began to scream and writhe in pretended pain. The experimenter said, "That's all right, he can take more. Give him some more." When the student turned the knob more, the subject would yell and scream harder and louder. Again the student looked up, and again the experimenter said, "That's all right. He can take more. Give it to him." A large percentage of students continued to turn the knob even though they could see and hear the apparent result of their own actions.

When the experiment was over, interviewers asked, "Why did you do it? Didn't you see the person was in pain?"

"Yes, I saw that," was the common answer.

"Why did you continue?"

The reply was simple: "It wasn't my experiment. After all, the psychologist was in charge. I figured he knew what he was doing, so I just followed what he said."

Any time one violates one's own conscience and values and engages in behavior that one does not consider right or conscionable or appropriate, one is in danger of taking a terrible trip to Abilene.

## Organizational Decisions to Fail

Trips to Abilene occur at the organization level, too. For example, a consultant to a large eastern corporation found that the company had committed several million dollars to the development of a new product. In interviewing almost all the top executives in the corporation, he discovered general concern about the multimillion-dollar research program, which represented an important corporate outlay. Each person said approximately the same thing: "I think the research program is a fiasco, an unwise investment of money. It isn't going to produce what we think it is."

"What are you going to do about it?"

"We just had a meeting, and we are going to commit another million-and-a-half to the research program." Each executive feared the consequences of speaking up and expressing his or her objections. Each thought that everybody else supported the project. As a result of this collective ignorance and fear, the corporation nearly took a trip to corporate bankruptcy in Abilene.

## Fear of Admitting the Truth

We find trips to Abilene at the corporate, family, and individual level. Why do they occur? What is it that causes people to marry people they don't love, take jobs they don't like, and support projects doomed to failure? Stated differently, why do they make decisions to fail? Underlying all such decisions are fear and fantasy—the fear of what might happen if one speaks up and voices the truth as he or she sees it. What will people say if we break our engagement? What will my wife say if I admit that I don't plan the kind of family life I think she wants? What will everyone say if I don't take the job in Chicago? What will happen to me if I declare that the last decision we made in our organization was dangerously speculative? What will happen to me if I reject a prevailing political opinion? The fear of what might happen, the fantasy of what might come tumbling down around us if we don't keep the peace, can put us in danger of taking a long, dusty trip to Abilene when we would much prefer to be in New Orleans.

## How to Avoid Trips to Abilene

Because decisions to fail often result from unawareness of the real feelings of others, it is important that someone risk expressing his or her concerns openly. Regardless of whether the setting is a business organization, a family, or a church, he or she must accept the consequences of his or her risk. Others, hearing this honest declaration of feelings, may be encouraged to overcome their own fears and fantasies. All may realize they are on a road none wants to travel and may take the opportunity to reverse their course in a direction they do want to take.

It is possible that the person raising the issue may find genuine disagreement with his or her concern, in which case he or she may set his or her fears to rest. There is also the possibility that the others are so afraid to reverse their previous decisions that they will react negatively to someone who has held up his or her secret fears for discussion and examination. Although he or she may be penalized or even rejected, at the same time he or she will be forced to move in directions that express an honest commitment.

## Implications for Managing Change

The consultants or change agents or managers who discover the dynamics of hidden agreement inherent in the Abilene paradox will serve their clients best by bringing together all parties and identifying areas of major agreement. They may even describe the Abilene parable and ask those present if the data they have gathered threatens such a possibility for them. The change agent then tries to help the client reduce the anxiety stemming from phantom fear and fantasies that block problem-solving, come to grips with decision making, and take the appropriate actions. In summary, by focusing on hidden agreements, the consultant helps his or her client reach conclusions destined to succeed rather than decisions sure to fail.

# CHAPTER 23

# The Consultation Process

Consulting with organizations regarding their improvement is a relatively new professional activity that produces organizational change. There are two types of consultants: "Outsiders," who come into the organization for a specified period, and "insiders," who are employed by the organization to work full-time as consultants. Although there are important differences between these roles, goals and methods are very similar. Both the consultant and the client should understand the processes of effective consulting to maximize the probability of success.

All consultants must build a relationship with the client and help the client plan for changes. These two activities—building a relationship and working for change—continue through all phases of the consulting process.

Much has been written about the role of the change agent, particularly from a theoretical point of view; however, the ongoing specifics of the change agent's work within an organization have not been as clearly set forth. This chapter addresses the strategies used by the outside consultant.

## Preliminary Consideration: Choosing the Consultant

Choosing a consultant is different than selecting a resource person, who is engaged to perform a particular function—to give a lecture, conduct a training problem, plan a workshop, or handle a team-building session. A consultant's role is different, especially when an organization requires assistance in problem identification. Because the diagnostic process is followed by development of a plan of action to solve the problem, a consultant must have a broader range of different skills than the resource person.

Consulting is always a human exchange. Even though he or she may deal with technical matters, the consultant, to be maximally effective, should have sufficient interpersonal skills to achieve the organization's goals without becoming entangled in problems with the client. The client should try to determine if the consultant has these interpersonal skills along with the ability to gather an appropriate range of data and identify problems and the experience to determine the actions needed to cope with the problems. Either the consultant or resource people may carry out the resulting plan of action.

The consultant is first and always an individual with values, habits, goals, attitudes, needs, and skills. Does this complexity of human attributes add up to the kind of person the client wants poking around in the organization? A consultant cannot help but be a role model for people in the client system watching how problems are uncovered and solved. The client would be well advised to gather data about the consultant regarding his or her personality as well as professional competence. Consultants who use the client to meet their own needs, whose values are not consistent with the values of the client system, who do not recognize their limitations, or who try to ingratiate themselves with clients rather than confront the issues probably do more harm than good.

Assuming the consultant also applied intelligence to the selecting of the client, let us look at the flow of activity between them.

## Phase 1: Initial Contact

In this example, the consultant was approached by the director of training and the director of public relations of a government agency. They asked if he was interested in establishing a development program for top management in their agency.

QUESTION 1. The first question that the consultant had to ask and answer for himself and the client was, "Am I capable of providing the kind of resource this particular client needs?" He told the two directors that he would be interested in working on such a program only if he was equipped to supply the development activity needed. This led to their next question.

QUESTION 2. "How can one determine just what training or development experience the management or client needs?"

This is not an easy question, for there are at least these three possibilities:

1. The agency might have objective needs that could be determined by an outside, impartial analysis. For example, an independent analysis might reveal too many managers with limited experience and a need for more managers with wide experience in other organizations. Such a need might not be identified through interviewing just managers.
2. Subjective needs of the management personnel may not be what is "objectively" needed. Managers' personal need for more recognition

and reward may not be as critical to the organization as new blood in the cadre of management.

3. It is possible that subjective and objective needs are fairly close.

It was agreed that a needs assessment would be conducted before making a final decision about the consultant's involvement. A needs assessment is data-gathering to determine what problems, concerns, and issues must be addressed if the organization is to improve its effectiveness.

## Phase 2: The Contract

Following the initial contact, the consultant establishes a "contract" with the client. Whether or not it is formalized and written, the contract is always psychological: it represents a set of expectations and understandings as to how the consultant will work. This contract may be reexamined and reformulated from time to time as the situation changes.

In this case, the consultant's basic contract specified that he would initiate a data-gathering process by interviewing all managers who would be involved in a development program, trying to be as objective as possible. He would tabulate and analyze the data, present it to the client, and determine on the basis of this information the problems that should be addressed. If the problems uncovered were outside the consultant's range of competency, his activity would end; if they were within his competency range, he would continue to work on planning and implementing action.

The consultant indicated immediately that if the agency's problems were in such areas as finance, budgeting, state-federal relations, or technical planning and programming peculiar to the work of that agency, then he would not be a good resource. If, however, their needs were in the area of interpersonal behavior or organizational structure, he felt he could be of assistance to them in designing and implementing a change plan.

## Phase 3: Data Collection: Entry and Relationship Development

From a strictly objective, scientific point of view, the collection of data should be conducted by someone who would not be involved in the program. Particularly when there is a possibility of profit, the consultant might distort the data. In this case, the objective method was not used because trained personnel for collecting data were not available and the work had to be done immediately in light of time and budget requirements.

The consultant decided to collect the data himself because he felt he could be suitably objective, and the client agreed.

**QUESTION 3.** "How can a consultant build a level of trust and confidence with the management and obtain the information necessary for an adequate diagnosis?"

The consultant knew that initial contacts are critical in terms of establishing a basis for an ongoing relationship. He therefore resolved to "level" with each person in the agency and explain his position and his goals.

The consultant felt that the interview process would be the most effective method to gather data and build relationships with the members of the client system with whom he would work. With each manager, he explained that he was not hired to undertake a total development program; he was trying to identify their needs and those of the agency in order to determine what kind of program, if any, would enhance productivity.

During the initial contact with members of the client system, the consultant works on two levels: 1) moving the task along; and 2) building relationships.

## Interview Questions

The following questions served as a general guide in each interview:

*a)* What is your job in the agency? Would you describe it to me?
*b)* What do you consider the biggest problems you face in doing your job?
*c)* What do you think you need personally to improve your functioning in your job?
*d)* What do you think are the biggest problems facing the agency?
*e)* What do you think would help the agency to function better?
*f)* What are the strengths of the agency as you see it?

The consultant felt free to question further within the areas raised in the initial questions. During each two-hour interview, the consultant was not only gathering information but also building relationships and establishing credibility important for future work. He also spent considerable time with the training director exploring the agency organization and its programs, policies, and procedures. Along with an employee attitude survey taken some eight years earlier, the consultant read the agency handbook and other literature describing its work.

The consultant then tabulated the data according to problems or needs mentioned in the interviews, listing all items of concern mentioned by three or more people.

# Phase 4: Data Presentation and Decision for Further Action

At a meeting of all top-level managers, the consultant presented the list of problems or concerns and pointed out areas in which he felt he could help and those that were not in his range of competency. The former areas included:

1. Dealing with conflict
2. Improving communications and feedback
3. Improving staff meetings and planning procedures
4. Improving the decision-making process
5. Widening the base of acceptance of each manager
6. Improving motivation

During the meeting, the consultant was considering the next question.

**QUESTION 4.** "How can I help the staff of this agency commit themselves to a program of change and development?"

Following the data presentation, the consultant advised the group to decide which issues concerned them and whether they wanted to follow a program in the areas of the consultant's competence. Before leaving, he indicated that he did not want pressure applied by the agency director, the training director, or others, and he assured them that they should decide what was best for the agency.

The next day the training officer reported to the consultant that after intense discussion, a set of issues was unanimously accepted in which all could participate; most of the issues fell in the consultant's area of competency. The group's decision undoubtedly was influenced by the relationship established with the consultant.

# Phase 5: The Development Program

At the decision-making meeting, the consultant had outlined a proposed development program within his areas of competence so the group would have some basis for making a decision about participation. The proposed program was as follows:

## Proposed Management and Organization Development Program

I. Initial Three-day Team Development Program

The purpose of this intensive period is to provide an opportunity for the group, which is essentially the top management team, to examine and begin to work on the following:

1. The level of acceptance of all team members
2. Level of communication among staff members
3. Staff decision-making procedures
4. Areas of conflict among staff members
5. The interpersonal competence level and management style of each staff member

New concepts of organization and management also would be introduced.

II. Individual Goal-Formation and Planning

Following the initial team-building phase, the consultant would meet with each participant to review feedback and recommendations and to help plan a program for his or her own improvement and the improvement of his or her department.

III. Follow-Up Consultation

The consultant, in collaboration with the internal training director, would meet with each manager and review plans and progress. A general meeting would be held in six months to review the program and determine future actions.

IV. Short Seminars

In addition to the follow-up consultations, seminars would be held to discuss problems of organization and management.

QUESTION 5. "What kind of training program would involve the members of the client system at a significant level?"

In discussions with the consultant, the agency administrator and the training director indicated that T-group or sensitivity group training was somewhat suspect among some of the management staff, and recommended that this format not be used. They were referring particularly to the completely unstructured T-group situation, which was considered applicable to the problems of the organization. The consultant agreed to forego unstructured situations and to center the three-day program on matters of concern to the staff members. A general team-building design seemed most appropriate in this situation.

The above design allowed the group to examine problem areas of concern to them. Because the first day was relatively structured and nonthreatening, the consultant was able to strengthen his relationship with the team and to watch them work together on structured issues. The exercises allowed everyone to examine the nature of problem-solving, planning, decision-making, conflict areas within the staff and level of acceptance of staff members, and to open channels of communication and feedback.

## Phase 6: The Follow-Up Program

**QUESTION 6.** "What type of follow-up activity will help implement the gains of the initial phase in the back-home situation?"

By its very nature, a team-building program conducted in-house among people who have ongoing relations has certain advantages; improvements in relationships are likely to continue. However, the consultant felt that each manager needed an opportunity to review the feedback given him or her during the first phase and to receive help in planning a program of improvement based on this new information.

During a discussion of management style and the feedback sessions that followed, the consultant took extensive notes on each person. He had a complete description of the person's self-perception and the staff's feedback to him or her. Within a month, the consultant began another series of interviews with each participant in which he reviewed the person's self-description and what others had shared in the way of feedback. Each person was asked, "In light of this information, what do you think you should be doing to improve your performance?" The consultant then tried to help devise a concrete plan for improvement.

Of critical importance were sessions with the top people in the agency, the administrator and assistant administrator, both of whom accepted the development program and openly supported all activities. Both received a great deal of feedback and developed plans to improve. Support from the top levels seemed to encourage others to give and receive feedback more openly and to plan optimistically for change.

## Phase 7: Termination

**QUESTION 7.** "How can the consultant leave the client organization after his or her work has ended?"

It is important that the relationship be terminated at a point where the client system has developed enough independence to continue a program of improvement without the consultant.

In this case, termination was not considered until each manager had a concrete plan for his or her own improvement; an intermediate progress report from the consultant had been circulated to the total staff; and a final written report outlining the program, gains made, and the work still to be done was distributed by the consultant.

At a formal termination session, the final report was reviewed and discussed before a closing dinner.

# Results of the Consultation

This development program does not include an evaluation of the program, which preferably should be made by someone not connected with the development activities and at some time following the termination of the consultant's work. Unfortunately, too few organizations' budget and program policies build in evaluation of programs. Thus, any evaluation of the aforementioned program can be very subjective at best.

In follow-up interviews with each manager, these improvements were commonly mentioned.

1. The administrator gained new insight into methods of decision making. In staff meetings, he now tried to arrive at a consensus for decisions that affected the total agency by involving those who would be affected by the decision.
2. People whose differences were explored in the feedback sessions continued to work on ways of resolving their conflicts.
3. Some managers made direct behavior changes, such as getting out of the office more and visiting others, consulting with others before making decisions, speaking up more in staff meetings, and taking more time to listen to subordinates.
4. Some employees had been able to clarify certain of their staff functions as a result of talking about their roles.
5. Certain of the younger and newer members of the management staff felt greater acceptance and more ease in the group and as a result felt freer to contribute in staff meetings.

These results indicate that use of a consultant can facilitate a change program in an organization. Management had concluded that no one in the organization had the time or expertise to see that a total development program was initiated and implemented. There were enough indicators that the agency's issues and problems warranted the hiring of a consultant. Throughout the program there was sufficient interaction between the consultant, the internal development people, and management to insure agreement on all actions by all involved parties.

# Bibliography

Allison, D. 1969. *The R & D Game*. Cambridge, Mass.:MIT Press.

Anderson, J. 1970. "Giving and Receiving Feedback." In *Organizational Change and Development*, ed. G. W. Dalton, P. R. Lawrence, and L. E. Greiner, pp. 339–346. Homewood, Ill.:Richard D. Irwin and Dorsey Press. Also in *Personnel Administration*, 31(1968):21–27.

Argyle, M; Gardner, G.; and Ciofi, F. 1958. "Supervisory Methods Related to Productivity, Absenteeism and Labour Turnover." *Human Relations* 11(February):24–25.

Argyris, C. 1957. *Personality and Organization*. New York:Harper and Row.

Argyris, C. 1962. *Interpersonal Competence and Organizational Effectiveness*. Homewood, Ill.:Richard D. Irwin and Dorsey Press.

Argyris, C. 1964. *Integrating the Individual and the Organization*. New York:Wiley.

Argyris, C. 1970. *Intervention Theory and Method*. Reading, Mass.:Addison-Wesley.

Argyris, C. 1971. *Management and Organizational Development*. New York:McGraw-Hill.

Bales, R. F. 1950. *Interaction Process Analysis*. Reading, Mass.:Addison-Wesley.

Barron, F. 1969. *Creative Person and Creative Process*. New York:Holt, Rinehart and Winston.

Beckhard, R. 1967. "The Confrontation Meeting." *Harvard Business Review* 45(2):149–155.

Beckhard, R. 1969. *Organization Development: Strategies and Models*. Reading, Mass.:Addison-Wesley.

Beckhard, R. 1972. "Optimizing Team-Building Efforts." *Journal of Contemporary Business* 1(3):23–32.

Beer, M. 1980. *Organization Change and Development*. Santa Monica:Goodyear.

Beer, M., and Huse, E. F. 1972. "A Systems Approach to Organization Development." *Journal of Applied Behavioral Science* 8:79–101.

Benjamin, A. 1969. *The Helping Interview*. New York:Houghton Mifflin.

Benne, K. D., and Sheats, P. 1948. "Functional Roles of Group Members." *Journal of Social Issues* 4(2):42–47.

Bennis, W. G. 1969. *Organization Development: Its Nature, Origins, and Prospects*. Reading, Mass.:Addison-Wesley.

Bennis, W. G.; Benne, K.; and Chin, R. 1969. *The Planning of Change*. New York:Holt, Rinehart and Winston.

Bennis, W. G., 1964. *Interpersonal Dynamics*. Homewood, Ill.:Dorsey Press.

Berne, E. 1964. *Games People Play*. New York:Grove Press.

Bigelow, J. 1982. "A Catastrophe Model of Organizational Change." *Behavioral Science* 27(1):12–41.

Blake, R. R., and Mouton, J. S. 1962. "The Instrumental Training Laboratory." In *Issues in Training*. Washington:National Training Laboratories, 61–77.

Blake, R. R., and Mouton, J. S. 1964. *The Managerial Grid.* Houston:Gulf.

Blake, R. R., and Mouton, J. S. 1968. *Corporate Excellence through Grid Organization Development.* Houston:Gulf.

Blake, R. R., and Mouton, J. S. 1976. *Consultation.* Reading, Mass.:Addison-Wesley.

Blake, R. R., and Mouton, J. S. 1978. *The New Managerial Grid.* Houston:Guif.

Boss, W. 1983. "Team Building and the Problem of Regression: The Personal Management Interview as an Intervention." *JABS,* 19(1):67–83.

Bowers, D. G. 1973. "OD Techniques and Their Results in 23 Organizations: The Michigan ICL Study." *Journal of Applied Behavioral Science* 9:21–43.

Bradford, L. P.; Benne, K. D.; and Gibb, J. R. 1964. *T-Group Theory and Laboratory Method Innovation in Re-education.* New York:Wiley.

Bunker, D. R. 1965. "Individual Applications of Laboratory Training." *Journal of Applied Behavioral Science* 1:131–148

Bunker, D. R., and Knowles, E. S. 1967. "Comparison of Behavioral Changes Resulting from Human Relations Training Laboratories of Different Lengths." *Journal of Applied Behavioral Science* 3:505–524.

Burke, W. W. 1971. "A Comparison of Management Development and Organization Development." *Journal of Applied Behavioral Science* 7:569–579.

Burke, W. W. 1976. "Organization Development in Transition." *Journal of Applied Behavioral Science* 12:22–43.

Burke, W. W. 1982. *Organization Development: Principles and Practices.* Boston: Little, Brown.

Burke, W. W., and Hornstein, H. A., eds. 1972. *The Social Technology of Organization Development.* La Jolla, Calif.:University Associates.

Burns, T., and Stalker, G. M. 1962. *The Management of Innovation.* Chicago:Quadrangle Books.

Campbell, J. P., and Dunnette, M. D. 1968. "Effectiveness of T-Group Experiences in Managerial Training and Development." *Psychological Bulletin* 70:73–104.

Cartwright, D., and Zander, A. 1960. *Group Dynamics: Research and Theory,* 2nd ed. New York:Harper and Row.

Coch, L., and French, J. R. P. 1948. "Overcoming Resistance to Change." *Human Relations* 1:512–532.

Cutler, B. R., and Dyer, W. G. 1965. "Initial Adjustment Processes in Young Married Couples." *Social Forces* 44, no. 2(December):195–201.

Dalton, G. 1970. Influence and Organizational Change." In *Organizational Change and Development,* ed. G. Dalton, P. Lawrence, and L. Greiner. Homewood, Ill.:Irwin-Dorsey.

Daughen, J. R., and Binzen, P. 1971. *The Wreck of the Penn Central.* Boston:Little, Brown.

Davis, S. A. 1967. "An Organic Problem-Solving Method of Organizational Change." *Journal of Applied Behavioral Science* 3:3–21.

Davis, S. M. 1982. "Transforming Organizations: The Key to Strategy." *Organizational Dynamics* 14(Winter):64–80.

Diedrich, R. C., and Dye, H. A. 1972. *Group Procedures: Purposes, Procedures, and Outcomes (Selected Readings for the Counselor).* Boston:Houghton Mifflin.

Dubin, R. 1965. *Leadership and Productivity.* San Francisco:Chandler.

Dyer, W. G. 1969. "Acceptance or Change." *Human Relations Training News* 13.

Dyer, W. G. 1972. *Modern Theory and Method in Group Training.* New York:Van Nostrand Reinhold.

Dyer, W. G. 1977. *Team Building: Issues and Alternatives.* Reading, Mass.:Addison-Wesley.

Dyer, W. G. 1978a. "What Makes Sense in Management Training." *Management Review* (Spring).

Dyer, W. G. 1978b. "When is a Problem a Problem?" *The Personnel Administrator* 23:6 (June).

Dyer, W. G. 1983. *Contemporary Issues in Management and Organizational Development.* Reading, Mass.:Addison-Wesley.

Dyer, W. G., and Urban, D. 1962. "Analyzing Marital Adjustment Using Role Theory." *Marriage and Family Living* 20(November):53–58.

Dyer, W. G., Jr. 1982. "Culture in Organizations: A Case Study and Analysis." Alfred P. Sloan School of Management Working Paper #1279-82 (February).

Festinger, L.; Rucker, H.; and Schachter, S. 1956. *When Prophecy Fails.* New York:Harper and Row.

Fiedler, F. 1965. "Engineer the Job to Fit the Manager." *Harvard Business Review* (September–October).

Fleishman, E. A., and Berniger J. 1960. "One Way to Reduce Office Turnover." *Personnel* 37 (May–June):63–69.

Fleishman, E. A., and Harris, E. F. 1962. "Patterns of Leadership Behavior Related to Employee Grievances and Turnover." *Personnel Psychology* 15:43–56.

Fordyce, J. K., and Weil, R. 1971. *Managing with People.* Reading, Mass.:Addison-Wesley.

Franklin, J. L. 1976. "Characteristics of Successful and Unsuccessful Organization Development." *Journal of Applied Behavioral Science* 12:471–492.

French, J. R. P., and Caplan, R. D. 1972. "Organizational Stress and Individual Strain." In A. Marion, *The Failure of Success.* New York:AMACOM.

French, W. L., and Bell, C. H. 1978. *Organization Development: Behavioral Science Interventions for Organization Improvement,* 2nd ed. Englewood Cliffs, N.J.:Prentice-Hall.

Galbraith, J. R. 1982. "Designing the Innovative Organization." *Organizational Dynamics,* 10(Winter):5–29.

Ghiselin, B., ed. 1952. *The Creative Process.* Berkeley:University of California Press.

Gibb, J. R. 1965. "Fear and Facade." In R. Farson, *Science and Human Affairs.* Palo Alto, Ca.:Science and Behavior Books.

Gibb, J. R. 1978. *Trust: A New View of Personal and Organizational Development.* Los Angeles:Guild of Tutors Press.

Goffman, E. 1959. *The Presentation of Self in Everyday Life.* Garden City, NY:Doubleday.

Golembiewski, R. T., and Blumberg, A. 1970. *Sensitivity Training and the Laboratory Approach.* Itasca, Ill.:F. E. Peacock.

Guest, R. H. 1962. *Organizational Change: The Effect of Successful Leadership Change.* Homewood, Ill.:Richard D. Irwin and Dorsey Press.

Hackman, J. R., and Oldham, G. R. 1980. *Work Redesign.* Reading, Mass.:Addison-Wesley.

Hall, J. 1976. "To Achieve or Not: The Manager's Choice." *California Management Review* 18(4):5–18.

Hall, J., and Williams, M. S. 1970. "Group Dynamics Training and Improved Decision Making." *Journal of Applied Behavioral Science* 6:39–68.

Harrison, R. 1972. "Role Negotiation: A Tough-minded Approach to Team Development." In *The Social Technology of Organization Development,* ed. W. W. Burke and H. A. Hornstein, pp. 84–96. La Jolla, Calif.:University Associates.

Harrison, R. 1981. "Startup: The Care and Feeding of Infant Systems." *Organizational Dynamics* 658.05(Summer):5–29.

Harvey, J. B. 1974. "The Abilene Paradox: The Management of Agreement." *Organizational Dynamics* 3(Summer):63–80.

Harvey, J.; Foltz, J.; and McLaughlin, J. 1974. "Organization Development: A Line Function." Washington, D.C. National Training Laboratories.

Hersey, P., and Blanchard, K. H. 1977. *Management of Organizational Behavior,* 3rd ed. Englewood Cliffs, N.J.:Prentice-Hall.

Herzberg, F. 1966. *Work and the Nature of Man.* Cleveland:World Publishing.

Herzberg, F. 1968a. "One More Time: How Do You Motivate Employees?" *Harvard Business Review* 46(1):53–62.

Herzberg, F. 1968b. "Motivation, Morale and Money." *Psychology Today* 1 (March).

Herzberg, F.; Mausner, B.; and Snyderman, B. 1959. *The Motivation to Work.* New York:Wiley.

Homans, G. 1961. *Social Behavior, Its Elementary Forms.* New York:Harcourt, Brace and World.

Hornstein, A. A.; Bunker, B. B.; Burke, W. W.; Gindes, M.; and Lewicki, R. J. 1971. *Social Intervention: A Behavioral Science Approach.* New York:The Free Press, Collier-Macmillan.

House, R., and Rizzo, J. 1972. "Role Conflict and Ambiguity as Critical Variables in a Model of Organizational Behavior." *Organization Behavior and Human Performance* 7(3):467–505.

Hunsaker, P. L., and Hunsaker, J. S. 1981. "Decision Styles—In Theory, In Practice." *Organizational Dynamics* 14(Autumn):23–36.

Huse, E. F. 1980. *Organization Development and Change*, rev. ed. St. Paul:West.

Jacobs, A., and Spradlin, W. 1974. *The Group as Agent of Change*. New York:Behavioral Publications.

Kahn, R. L., and Katz, D. 1960. "Leadership Practices in Relation to Productivity and Morale." In *Group Dynamics*, ed. D. Cartwright and A. Zander. Evanston, Ill.:Row, Peterson.

Kahn, R. L.; Wolfe, D. M.; Quinn, R. P.; Snoek, J. D.; and Rosenthal, R. A. 1964. *Organizational Stress: Studies in Role Conflict and Ambiguity*. New York:Wiley, especially part 6, "Conflict and Attempted Solution."

Kast, Fremont. 1980. "Scanning the Future Environment: Social Indicators." *California Management Review* 13(1):22–31.

Katz, D., and Kahn, R. L. 1978. *The Social Psychology of Organizations*, 2nd ed. New York:Wiley.

Keenan, V.; Kerr, W.; and Sherman, W. 1951. "Psychological Climate and Accidents in an Automotive Plant." *Journal of Applied Psychology* 35(April):89–91.

Kelman, H. C. 1961. "Process of Opinion Change." *Public Opinion Quarterly* 25(Spring):57–78.

Kluckhohn, F. R., and Strodtbeck, F. L. 1961. *Variations in Value Orientations*. Evanston, Ill.:Row, Peterson.

Latham, G. P.; Cummings, L. L.; and Mitchell, T. R. 1981. "Behavioral Strategies to Improve Productivity." *Organizational Dynamics* 9(Winter):5–23.

Lawrence, P. R., and Lorsch, J. W. 1967. *Organization and Environment: Managing Differentiation and Integration*. Boston:Division of Research, Harvard Business School.

Leontiades, M. 1980. "The Dimensions of Planning: In Large Industrialized Organizations." *California Management Review* 22(4):82–86.

Letterer, J. 1973. *The Analysis of Organizations*. New York:Wiley.

Lewicki, R. J. 1981. "Organizational Seduction: Building Commitment to Organizations." *Organizational Dynamics* 14 (Autumn):5–21.

Lewin, K. 1951. *Field Theory in Social Science*. New York:Harper.

Lewin, K. 1958. "Group Decision and Social Change." In *Readings in Social Psychology*, ed. E. E. Maccoby, T. M. Newcomb, and E. L. Hartley, pp. 197–211. New York:Holt, Rinehart and Winston.

Lieberman, M. A.; Yalom, I.D.; and Miles, M. B. 1973. *Encounter Groups: First Facts*. New York:Basic Books.

Likert, R. 1961. *New Patterns of Management*. New York:McGraw-Hill.

Likert, R. 1967. *The Human Organization*. New York:McGraw-Hill.

Lippitt, R.; Watson, J.; and Westley, B. 1958. *Dynamics of Planned Change*. New York:Harcourt, Brace.

Mann, F. C. 1965. "Toward an Understanding of the Leadership Role in Formal Organization." In R. Dubin, *Leadership and Productivity*, pp. 68–103. San Francisco:Chandler.

Marrow, A. 1972. *The Failure of Success*. New York:AMACOM.

Marrow, A. J.; Bowers, D. G.; and Seashore, S. E. 1967. *Management by Participation*. New York:Harper and Row.

Maslow, A. H. 1943. "A Theory of Human Motivation." *Psychological Review* 50:370–396.

Maslow, A. H. 1954. *Motivation and Personality*. New York:Harper and Brothers.

McClelland, D. C. 1975. *Power, the Inner Experience*. New York:Wiley.

McGregor, D. 1960. *The Human Side of Enterprise*. New York:McGraw-Hill.

McGregor, D. 1967. *The Professional Manager*. New York:McGraw-Hill.

Meyer, H. H. 1972. "Feedback that Spurs Performance." In *The Failure of Success*, ed. A. Marrow. New York:AMACOM, 199–216.

Miles, R. E., and Snow, C. C. 1978. *Organizational Strategy, Structure, and Process*. New York:McGraw-Hill.

Molsar, J. J., and Rogers, D. L. 1979. "The Design of Alternatives in Organizational Conflict." *Administrative Science Quarterly* 29:405–422.

Nadler, D. A. 1977. *Feedback and Organization Development: Using Data-Based Methods*. Reading, Mass.:Addison-Wesley.

Nadler, D. A. 1981. "Managing Organizational Change: An Integrative Perspective." *Journal of Applied Behavioral Science* 17(2).

Nadler, D. A.; Mirvis, P. H.; and Cammann, C. 1976. "The Ongoing Feedback System: Experimenting with a New Managerial Tool." *Organizational Dynamics* 4(4):63–80.

O'Reilly, III, C. A., and Weitz, B. A. 1983. "Managing Marginal Employees: The Use of Warnings and Dismissals." *Administrative Science Quarterly* (December):467–482.

Ouchi, W. G. 1981. *Theory Z*. Reading, Mass.:Addison-Wesley.

Ouchi, W. G., and Prince, R. L. 1978. "Hierarchies, Clans, and Theory Z: A New Perspective on Organization Development." *Organizational Dynamics* 7(2):25–44.

Passmore, W. G. 1982. "Overcoming the Road Blocks in Work Restructuring Efforts." *Organizational Dynamics* 14(Spring):54–67.

Pettigrew, A. M. 1979. "On Studying Organizational Cultures." *Administrative Science Quarterly* 24:570–581.

Pfeiffer, W., and Jones J. 1969–1974. *Structured Experiences for Human Relations Training*, vols. 1–5. Iowa City:University Associated Press.

Pickhardt, C. F. 1981. "Problems Posed by a Changing Organizational Membership." *Organizational Dynamics*, 658.05(Summer):69–80.

Porras, J. I. 1979. "The Comparative Impact of Different OD Techniques and Intervention Intensities." *Journal of Applied Behavioral Science* 15:156–178.

Porras, J. I., and Anderson, B. 1981. "Improving Managerial Effectiveness Through Modeling Based Training." *Organizational Dynamics* 9(Spring):60–77.

Porras, J. I., and Patterson, K. 1979. "Assessing Planned Change." *Group and Organization Studies* 4:39–58.

Porras, J. I., and Wilkens, A. 1980. "Organization Development in a Large System: An Empirical Assessment." *Journal of Applied Behavioral Science* 16:506–534.

Pryor, M., and Bass, B. 1959. "Some Effects of Feedback on Behavior in Groups." *Sociometry* 22(1):56–63.

Reisel, J. 1962. "Observations on the Trainer Role: A Case Study." *Leadership and Organization: A Behavioral Approach*. New York:McGraw-Hill. Reprinted in *Issues in Training*. Washington:National Training Laboratories, pp. 93–108.

Roethlisberger, F. J., and Dickson, W. J. 1939. *Management and the Worker*. Cambridge, Mass.:Harvard University Press.

Rogers, C. 1961. *On Becoming a Person*. Boston:Houghton-Mifflin.

Ross, I. C., and Zander, A. C. 1957. "Need Satisfaction and Employee Turnover." *Personnel Psychology* 10(Autumn):327.

Rothe, H. 1960. "Does Higher Pay Bring Higher Productivity?" *Personnel* 37(July-August):20–27.

Schein, E. H. 1969. *Process Consultation: Its Role in Organization Development*. Reading, Mass.:Addison-Wesley.

Schein, E. H. 1980. *Organizational Psychology*, 3rd ed. Englewood Cliffs, N.J.:Prentice-Hall.

Schein, E. H. 1981. SMR Forum, "Does Japanese Management Style Have a Message for American Managers?" *Sloan Management Review* 23:55–68.

Schein, E.; Bennis, W.; and Beckhard, R. 1969. *Organization Development Series*. Reading, Mass.:Addison-Wesley.

Schein, E. H., and Bennis, W. 1965. *Personal and Organizational Change Through Group Methods: The Laboratory Approach*. New York:Wiley.

Schwartz, H., and Davis, S. M. 1981. "Matching Corporate Culture and Business Strategy." *Organizational Dynamics* (Summer):30–48.

Steele, F. 1975. *Consulting for Organization Change*. Amherst:University of Massachusetts Press.

Steiner, G. 1965. *The Creative Organization*. Chicago:University of Chicago Press.

Tannenbaum, A. S. 1966. *Social Psychology of the Work Organization*. Belmont, Ca.:Wadsworth, especially Chapter 4, "Personal Adjustment and Conflict in the Work Organization."

Tavis, C. 1982. "Anger Defused." *Psychology Today* 16(11):25–35.

Thibaut, J. W., and Coules, J. 1952. "The Role of Communications in the Reduction of

Interpersonal Hostility." *Journal of Abnormal and Social Psychology* 47:770–777.

Tichy, N. M. 1982. "Managing Change Strategically: The Technical, Political, and Cultural Keys." *Organizational Dynamics* (Fall).

Timm, P. R. 1982. "Let's Not Have a Meeting!" Reprint from *Supervisory Management*. AMACOM (August).

Van Maanen, J. and Schein, E. H. 1979. "Toward a Theory of Organizational Socialization." In *Research in Organizational Behavior*, Vol. 1, ed. B. Staw, pp. 209–264. Greenwich, Conn.:JAI Press.

Vroom, V. H., and Yetton, P. W. 1973. *Leadership and Decision Making*. Pittsburgh:University of Pittsburgh Press.

Walker, C. R. 1957. *Toward the Automatic Factory*. New Haven:Yale University Press.

Walton, R. 1969. *Interpersonal Peace Making: Confrontations and Third Party Consultation*. Reading, Mass.:Addison-Wesley.

Weisbord, M. R. 1978. *Organizational Diagnosis: A Workbook of Theory and Practice*. Reading, Mass.:Addison-Wesley.

Weschler, I. R., and Reisel, J. 1960. *Inside a Sensitivity Training Group*. Los Angeles:Institute of Industrial Relations, University of California.

White, R., and Lippitt, R. 1968. "Leader Behavior and Member Reaction in Three 'Social Climates.' " In D. Cartwright and A. Zander, *Group Dynamics*. New York:Harper and Row.

Whyte, W. F. 1948. *Human Relations in the Restaurant Industry*. New York:McGraw-Hill.

Whyte, W. F. 1955. *Money and Motivation*. New York:Harper and Row

Whyte, W. F. 1961. *Men at Work*. Homewood, Ill.:Dorsey Press, pp. 125–135.

Wolfe, D., and Snork, J. D. 1962. "A Study of Tensions and Adjustment Under Role Conflict." *Journal of Social Issues* 18(3):102–121.

Woodman, R. W., and Sherwood, J. J. 1980. "Effects of Team Development Intervention: A Field Experiment." *Journal of Applied Behavioral Science* 16(2):211–227.

Yankelovich, D. 1981. *New Rules: Searching for Self Fulfillment in a World Turned Upside Down*. New York:Random House.

Zajonc, R. 1962. "Effects of Feedback and Probability of Group Success on Individual and Group Performance." *Human Relations* 15(2):149–161.

Zierden, W. E. 1980. "Leading Through the Follower's Point of View." *Organizational Dynamics* 14(Spring):27–45.

# Index